FREELANCE WRITING GUIDE

What to Expect in Your First Year as A Freelance Writer

Christine Rice

Freelance Writing Guide

By Christine Rice

ISBN-13: 978-1492202059

ISBN-10: 1492202053

Other books by Christine Rice:

Poetry for the Heart

Essays for the Soul

My Not-So-Ordinary Life

This book is dedicated to all new and experienced writers in the world who wish to become freelance writers.

Table of Contents

Introduction

First of all, thank you for showing interest in my book! I started writing *Freelance Writing Guide* after I had been a freelance writer for nine months and I finished it at sixteen months. I was initially inspired to write it because of all I had learned as a freelance writer and how much I enjoyed writing. I wanted to share what I had learned - both my experiences and my knowledge - with other writers to save them time from having to do the research (about content websites, writing book reviews, and search engine optimization, for example) on their own.

When I first began freelance writing, I had a lot of questions: How do the content websites work? What do the different types of "rights" to a writer's work mean?

What is the proper structure of a book review? Is it necessary to brainstorm ideas and create an outline? I hope, by the end of this book, these and other questions will be answered. I hope that you will feel more prepared to take the plunge into starting a freelance writing career.

This book is written objectively as a factual book that is addressed directly to you as a reader, so I'd like to tell you a little about myself to share my personal and professional experiences with you so that you will know the type of person I am and what qualifies me to write this book.

I had wanted to be a writer since 2005, which was when I bought my first computer. I wrote journal entries and poetry since 1990, but I wanted to get more serious about my writing and thought a computer would help me do so. So I began typing poems and essays on the computer.

In 2006, I read a book about a woman's experiences with losing weight that she initially chronicled in a weekly magazine column. She was living a life she chose and writing about it for a career.

It was at that moment I realized I could do the same, so I decided I would become a professional writer.

I began writing a book about eating healthy and weight loss, and I queried twenty literary agents. No one picked up my book idea, but I wasn't discouraged. I tried writing my book again from the beginning to make it better, but didn't end up finishing either version.

In 2007, I enrolled in college as an English major. I truly loved school and did my schoolwork perfectly, because I had a passion for it. I thought, this is my ticket to succeeding as a writer! A few months later, I joined Writing.com, where I created a portfolio for the poems and essays I had written and got involved in the website's online community.

That same year, I published my first book, *Poetry for the Heart*, as a paperback with Lulu. I liked the feeling of being published and holding a book of my writing, so in 2008 I published a second book, *Essays for the Soul*. I quickly began writing my third book, which was an autobiography.

In 2009, I tried writing for Helium, where I published a few poems and essays. I also signed up with Demand Studios (content website) and Textbroker (ghostwriting marketplace). But I quickly got discouraged, because I thought the pay was very little (I mistakenly thought writers made a lot of money from the start).

That same year, I published the autobiography and titled it *My Not-So-Ordinary Life*. I continued to work on school while working full-time as a finance assistant. I was very busy and couldn't wait to become a professional writer.

Unfortunately, I stopped attending school at the end of 2009, because I lacked motivation, and I also resigned from my job in finance.

For a little over a year, I dealt with health issues from a car accident. I started a health blog at the end of 2010 and blogged regularly.

In the spring of 2011, I was feeling better health-wise and had more time on my hands, so I decided to give those content websites another try. I put all my time and effort into writing articles and poems for

Helium, Textbroker, Yahoo, and Suite101. I also worked for Elance and submitted over a dozen proposals to open positions, but unfortunately I was not selected for any; however, I did learn a lot about writing proposals and how the work-for-hire community works.

In December 2011, I began writing book reviews for publishers and authors. I wrote a book review for every book I read. (I think I will always do that, because I enjoy reading, and writing a book review doesn't take up much of my time, generally speaking.)

In January 2012, I began writing this book and another book, published second editions of my three published books, started an author blog, and really committed myself to writing full-time. From January up until April 2012—my one year anniversary as a freelance writer—I learned how to compose a press release (and wrote several), took up marketing (by hosting online events), participated in blog interviews, wrote guest blog posts, and provided editing services.

From April 2012 up until now, well, that will be saved for a future book about what to expect in the *second* year of a freelance writing career!

In this book, there are no untrue claims that you'll be rich from day one, and none of the information is exaggerated in any way. Rather, the information provided is truthful and direct about what I encountered in my first year as a freelance writer.

I truly hope you enjoy this book. I also hope it answers your questions and you learn a lot. All the best to you!

Sincerely,

Christine Rice

8/12/12

PART 1

WRITING AND PUBLISHING

Chapter 1
Write a Lot and Create a Portfolio

So you're interested in becoming a freelance writer? There is a lot to learn, but we'll take it a step at a time and divulge each important point a chapter at a time.

First, you'll need to address your priorities. Have you started writing yet? Writing is crucial to being a freelance writer. When you break it down, a freelance writer is a writer that makes money off of their writing (while working from home). You can perform the act of writing without earning money, such as if you don't publish it, but as a freelance writer you can't earn money without the act of writing. Therefore, the most basic and important component of freelance writing is writing.

How to Write

Teaching someone how to compose a piece of writing is similar to how animals care for their young. They feed and nurture them, and teach them skills, and then, probably when the child animal still doesn't feel very independent yet, the parent animal lets them go fend for themselves. Let me explain.

Writing is taught in school in English classes. In college, it is taught through more specialized classes, such as creative writing and technical writing. You will have received lots of instruction on mechanics, vocabulary, spelling, structure, and grammar in school, and possibly tips on conciseness, forms, research, and creativity in college. Then you are set free to do it all on your own and, hopefully, remember what you've learned. It doesn't end there. There is more to learn, more practice to gain, and more avenues to explore.

Unless you are an English teacher, it is difficult to teach someone how to write. This is especially true for writers, because writing techniques come more naturally to them, so they find it hard to explain how they do what they do. Teaching writing is partially an abstract topic, as every person has their own preferences on what makes good writing.

Read books to educate yourself on writing skills. You can teach yourself how to write or how to improve your writing, and you will be your best teacher. Just observing how authors use language, grammar, and punctuation, will teach you correct writing technique. But also, be aware that not every author knows and uses writing techniques perfectly in every sentence. An author has a little room for preference and creative expression.

The rules of writing have not changed much in the last 100 years, so it's a good idea to at least learn basic writing skills. *The Elements of Style* by William Strunk and E.B. White will be helpful.

Finding Ideas

To pick a topic to write about, go online and search "writing prompts." (Writing prompts are a sentence or two that can spark creativity and get you writing.) Browse the websites in your search, and scan through the writing prompts they have, until you find one that interests you or compels you to write. You can write about anything, so there are many things to write about! Once you have a topic, choose a medium (essay, short story, poem, etc.) and create your masterpiece.

Writing Mediums

It is a good idea to try out different writing mediums, because it is most beneficial to know how to create several types of writing, such as articles, blog posts, novels, web content, reports, sales letters, and so on. Try what appeals to you and learn about the rest. The more writing mediums you can create, the more freelance writing jobs you will qualify for.

Just do it—Write!

Now, you know how to write, and it can and will improve by using your skills to express yourself on the page. Write what comes to mind, write a song, write a poem, write a short story— just write, every day.

If you do not write every day, you will get rusty and won't feel like picking up the pen or typing. Even if you can only manage a paragraph, make that your goal, and write it down. When you do so, you will likely write more than that one paragraph. Encouraging your thoughts to flow, by trying to write, will often open a dam and the words will come pouring out onto the page. The hardest part is *starting* to write.

Writing is work, and even though you love it, it is still hard and will be viewed as work. But if you set aside some time each day to write something, you will be more productive and will write better, because you've unleashed your creative juices. It will be much easier to make your way over to the keyboard or paper if you are already in the habit of doing so. Just do it. Don't let yourself talk yourself out of writing.

Seeing Your Words in Print

It is rewarding to see your words on paper (or on the computer screen), no matter how many or how few words are there. You have triumphed and accomplished, and that feeling is a reward that you need to treasure and remember the next time you consider writing. Writing feels good, especially to a writer.

Creating a Portfolio

As a freelance writer you will do a lot of writing, especially in the beginning, because you'll need to establish a portfolio. A portfolio is what will help you get more freelance work.

The portfolio does not have to be published clips. Quality written pieces that you have saved on your computer can act as writing samples.

Your portfolio will be forever changing as new writing is added, pieces are revised, and some are discarded. So, how do you go about creating a substantial writing portfolio? Write.

Start with the basics by putting yourself at the keyboard or at a pad of paper as often as you feel inspired or at least once a day if possible. You will eventually end up at the keyboard, because everything ends up typed. But, maybe you like to begin by writing longhand first, for it makes you feel more creative and "free" with your words. Or, maybe you are efficient, or never wrote anything out by hand, except lists, so it is more natural for you to write everything at the computer.

You might also find that you like to switch between the notepad and the computer, because a variety of writing approaches helps motivate you. Decide on what works for you in the moment. Flexibility spurs creativity, which is very good for writers.

Create as many quality writing pieces as you can and add them to a portfolio, either an online one, such as on Behance or Writing.com, or a plastic or canvas portable one, or both. You may not earn much money from these writings, but you'll be building a portfolio and improving your writing skills, which is necessary to advance your career.

Writing Communities

You can join a writing community to participate in writing contests, post your writing for critique, and meet fellow writers. Writing.com is a website for writers that has writing prompts and motivates and inspires writers to write through contests, groups, and activities. Being around other writers helps, because you have things in common, and you will be able to share your accomplishments with others like you.

Writer's Digest Community has a forum of thousands of discussions, blog posts, pages for the different genres with helpful and specific information on each page, numerous groups that exist around a central theme, a profile page for each member, the ability to get writing critiqued, and more.

Get motivated. Get involved. Join a writing community.

Making a Career from Writing

Wanting to make a career from your writing is why you are here reading this book. You want to take what you enjoy most and make money from doing it. It's understandable and a very wise decision. Some people never find out what they enjoy the most. If they do, they are sometimes unable to make a career out of it, for different reasons. But you've discovered your talent and passion, and want to pursue it.

Work is so much easier when you truly enjoy what you do. Believe it or not, you will *want* to work, all the time, and people will think you're crazy for working so much. But you'll be happy, which is one of the most important aspects of life.

What to Expect from This Book

This book will teach you all that you need to know about your first year as a freelance writer, so that you can be prepared and knowledgeable when you take the first steps. You will be able to learn from someone who has gone before you. You don't have to take a leap of faith. Rather, you will be educated and able to decide the best route to take to make your dreams become a reality.

Success may not happen right away, because earning a living as a freelance writer takes lots of preparation and practice. You have to work your way to the top with experience. But don't let that disappoint you, because it is achievable. It will just take education and effort to make it happen. Becoming an established freelance writer is definitely worth the effort. It's much better than doing something that doesn't appeal much to you.

Make it happen. Put in effort and you will reap the benefits. In the meantime, there are many steps to take and much to do. So let's get started!

Chapter 2

Write for an Online Audience

Now that you have a portfolio of writing samples, you'll likely want to publish them and earn some royalties. As a new writer, or at least new to publishing, publishing your writing online is a great step. For one, you get published, which is personally rewarding. Second, you can earn a few dollars or more from the websites you publish on, which is better than earning nothing if you were to leave your work sitting in your portfolio. Third, you can build name recognition and a presence on the Web. Fourth, and most important, is that your work is published and you can provide links to your work when you apply for writing positions or freelance work, or try to get published in print.

Therefore, online publishing is a great stepping stone to other opportunities.

In addition, you can even earn a living just from online publishing by selecting higher and higher paying opportunities on websites that you will publish with.

Before publishing, you must compose your writing. Writing for the Web has its own style and method. In general, the writing is more conversational and direct than in print. Online writing mediums have different formats and techniques. First, let's cover article writing.

Writing and Formatting Online Articles

To give a general description of what an online article on the Internet looks like, for those who haven't perused content websites or articles on the Web, it is similar to what a textbook page looks like—lots of pictures (or, in this case, ads), color, subtitles, text formatting, and separate content boxes) than like an academic essay (plain text with indenting paragraphs). In addition, online articles are "broken up" with lists and bullets. A blank line is put between each paragraph instead of indenting (which are called "block paragraphs"), and the paragraphs are shorter and, ideally, have bold subtitles, in order to make the article easy to read and more likely that it will be read in its entirety.

Online articles are typically constructed like this: Title, introduction paragraph, subtitle, body paragraph 1, subtitle, body paragraph 2, subtitle, body paragraph 3, and conclusion paragraph. The introduction paragraph starts with a sentence that grabs the reader's attention, followed by one or two sentences that provide an overview of the topic, and then one sentence that "leads" the reader into the body of the article.

There are always *at least* three body paragraphs, and they are to be in a logical order. Each paragraph is its own idea and doesn't usually need transitions, because the subtitles let the reader know what is coming next. In addition, like mentioned above, there can also be numbered lists or bullet points in the body of the article for organization purposes and ease of readability.

The conclusion provides or summarizes the point of the article and has a sentence that "wraps up" (i.e. finalizes/brings to a close) the article.

Online articles must engage the audience, hold the reader's attention, and be written clearly and concisely. Most are direct and to-the-point, like most nonfiction, rather than descriptive and creative. The article's structure—both the formatting and writing style—should effectively "lead" the reader through the article from the first sentence to the last sentence.

Publishing Poetry Online

The only difference with publishing poetry online is that the poems are typically shorter than in print. That means the poems are concise, engaging, and interesting, and the language "moves" the reader through the poem quickly by being entertaining and progressive. Haiku poetry is often published online, because the format of the poem is only three lines.

Where to Publish Online

The short answer is on your blog or a content website. There are other places you can publish, but those are the most effective when you are new to publishing your writing. Let's go over them separately and in more detail.

Blog

Every writer needs their own blog. A blog is a webpage to record entries (i.e. blog posts) of events, experiences, and thoughts, and to share knowledge and advice. Blog posts are visible to everyone on the Web, so it's possible that anyone can read them.

Because blogs require a more casual writing style, like most online mediums, it might be easy to think of a blog as a personal diary; but you should not reveal too much personal information as a freelance writer, because it is a reflection of you as a professional. Freelance writing is a career and should be taken as such.

A blog is a way to gain a readership and build a relationship with your readers, so blog posts should also be personable. Ideally, you'll want to build a credible reputation *and* loyal readers of your work, so it is recommended to be both professional and personable in your blog posts.

The main way to earn income from your blog is by having advertisements on your blog—either Google ads or affiliate ads. Keep in mind that you only earn money if your blog visitors click on your ads and/or buy something afterwards. It's okay to use a few ads, but be selective. It is best that they relate to the theme of your blog so they fit the blog more naturally (and you'll get more clicks). Don't go overboard with advertisements, because if your blog is full of flashy ads, it will scare away your readers.

You can sign up for affiliate ads online through Google Affiliate, Amazon Associates, or ClickBank. Then do a search for products that match your blog's theme, apply to be an affiliate, and then copy and paste the ad code into an HTML text box through your blog's account. (More about earning income from ads in chapter 21.)

A blog is mostly for being a publishing platform for your writing, to gain a readership, and to get your name out into the online world. So rather than considering using blogging as a main income source, it is best to think of it as more of a gift to your readers. More opportunities will come your way with that outlook. But there's no reason why it can't be profitable as well.

Content Website

On content websites, you can publish articles, poems, short stories, and more. Each of these websites has a large amount of published articles (some writers publish hundreds of articles, and there are thousands of writers on each website) and the website doesn't pay the writers much (likely because of the massive number of articles they have to account for).

The good news is that it is *not* extremely difficult to get published with a content website, you can earn some money, you can acquire published writing samples, and you can gain experience. You can also learn how to write effective web content for an online audience.

Some content websites:

- Yahoo! Contributor Network
- Helium
- Constant Content
- EZine Articles
- Wikinut
- Suite101
- Demand Media Studios

- About.com
- HubPages
- Bright Hub
- Examiner

Most content websites require an application and a writing sample before they will approve your membership. Some automatically approve the memberships and so you can begin to write and publish right away. Others review your application and contact you with their decision of whether or not you can write for them. Essentially, when you join or get approved to write for these websites—they are all free to join and write for, by the way—you will learn their writing style requirements and guidelines. Then you will submit your first article. With some of the websites, the first few articles a new writer submits will be reviewed by editorial staff to make sure you are familiar with their guidelines and that your work is publishable.

Once you get through the review process, you can publish your writing at a faster rate. Many of these websites have “assignments” or article titles you can claim and write for.

Get as much of your work published with these websites as possible. Often it is good to have 100 or more published items before moving on to the next step with publishing: submitting to periodicals.

Chapter 3

Traditional Publishing with Periodicals

Now that you've accumulated a writing portfolio with published writing samples, you can dip your toes into the traditional publishing fountain.

A warning: don't be surprised if you don't get published right away, and don't be fazed by rejections. Traditional publishing is hard to break into, but it *can* be done. Likely, you'll need to submit your writing to many different publications before it will be published. But once you get used to querying publications, and once you learn how to tailor your writing to the publication's style and audience, you will find you are published more often and may even become a regular freelance writer for a publication.

There is a tough competition for staff writing positions at magazines, but there are many opportunities for freelancers. Some magazines receive up to 90 percent of their content from freelance writers. The magazines do, however, get lots of submissions, so it's your job to make yours stand out by having a unique idea that is fitting for the magazine, written in a style that is similar to what they usually publish, and represented by a stunning query letter that gets the editor's attention and makes you look like the perfect person to write the article.

It's not easy to get published in a magazine, but it is possible, and in time you will get better at it.

Unique Article Angle

It is important to have a unique angle to the article idea that you submit to a magazine. Magazines don't publish two articles with the same idea within two or more years of each other. Wouldn't you remember, if you were a regular subscriber to a magazine, a prior article on the same idea if it was published one year later? That is why magazines like it when creative-thinking writers come up with inventive article ideas for their magazine. Plus, magazines need a variety of articles to appeal to readers. That is why there are always opportunities for freelance writers from different backgrounds.

Brainstorm Ideas

As a writer, the best way to come up with article ideas is to brainstorm. In other words, sit at your desk, take a couple of deep breaths and exhales, and begin thinking about the main topic of the magazine. Then ask yourself a few questions about the magazine's topic to get your mind thinking: What do you know about the topic? What would you like to know about it? What interests you about it? What experiences have you had with it? Then write down every idea that comes to mind, and as you do, you will naturally come up with more ideas, like a "domino effect" (the brain is an idea and thought factory that is always working, contrary to what some people believe in regards to writer's block).

Narrow Your Idea

From your brainstormed list of ideas, take your favorite idea and mold it into a title, by re-wording and revising it. Then make it specific and detailed. For instance, if your initial idea was "rabbit communication," and you made the preliminary title "Can rabbits communicate?", to make it a more specific and effective title, you might change it to: "How do rabbits communicate their dietary needs to their owners?" By adding "dietary needs" and "owners" to the title, the topic is narrower and more suitable for an article length of up to 2,000 words.

Fitting for the Magazine

It is important to make sure your article topic fits the magazine's style and audience. For style, consider if it is casual or reserved, personal or professional, fun or serious. Also identify the topic of the magazine (e.g. horses, crafts, home improvement, etc.) and the average demographics of the audience (i.e. class, gender, age, etc.). To make sure your idea is fitting for the magazine, view the magazine online or buy an issue at the store, and read through the magazine, paying attention to the writing style and topics covered, and observing the advertisements for the magazine topic and audience demographics. Learn as much as you can about the magazine that you wish to submit to.

Effective Querying

Before starting to write your query letter, you must first obtain the name and address of the editor to submit your query letter to. You can find this information online under "contact us" or "submission guidelines," or by calling the company and politely asking, as well as asking for the correct spelling of the editor's name and their prefix (Mr. or Mrs.) if it's not clear. You also need to read the submission guidelines for the correct method of composing and submitting your query letter.

Now you will draft your query letter. There is a certain technique for writing them:

1. *Start with a "hook," which can be an interesting fact or a question.* Make it lively and compelling so that the editor will want to read more.
2. *Explain your article topic and show how it's interesting.* Tell the editor why your idea is fitting for their magazine and its audience, and how it is unique but important.

3. *Briefly state your credentials.* What experience do you have with the topic? What have you published already on the topic? What education do you have that is relevant? On that note, make sure to include your resume (if you have professional credentials and education) and published clips (or a list of website links to your online published writing).
4. *Include a call to action.* Tell the editor that you look forward to hearing their thoughts about your article idea, and provide your contact information and when you can best be reached.

It is fine to call the editor a couple of weeks later to make sure they didn't misplace your query letter and to find out their thoughts on it. Do not repeatedly call, though, and if the editor decides they do not want to give you the article assignment, do not try to convince them otherwise. Politely say, "thank you for your time," and move on to query another magazine.

Also consider, there is not much room for compromising when you are a newly published writer. The most you can do is submit your best ideas, hope for the best, and if they want to hire you for the assignment, accept their offer. Once you have written several articles for a magazine, you can inquire about regular freelance assignments and higher pay.

Rejection

All writers get rejection slips. There is not one writer in the world that gets every idea, article, and book accepted for publication. No one is that perfect. Therefore, rejections are part of being a writer. Write your best work, spend time editing and proofreading, submit your best queries, give a word of encouragement to the editor, learn from constructive criticism you receive, and continue writing.

As you can see, writing and publishing is a large cycle. If you wish to be a part of it, you must be okay with receiving rejections. It's not a personal attack, and if you put your best work forward, it's not even an attack on your idea or writing style. What you submit to the editor may or may not be right for them *at that time*. There are lots of writers in the world and only a few spots for publication. So you will not get published every time. But the times you do get published will make it all seem worthwhile.

Acceptance

If your idea is accepted, congratulations! When your article is accepted, you are granting the publication (at a minimum) "one-time rights," which means that you give the publication the right to publish your work once and then you are free to resubmit the article to other publications.

If the publication requests more rights to your work, and sometimes they will, you will have to approve the contract in the form of an email or a letter that you will sign and send back. Be careful what rights to your work you give away. You can change the contract by persuasion, but as a new writer you will most likely accept the terms of the contract, unless the publisher demands all rights to your work, then you may decide not to sign the contract and take your work elsewhere.

There is a little room for compromise with contracts. Knowing what the terms mean will help you decide what is best for you. The following is a list of writers' rights and descriptions for each (information obtained from *Writer's Market 2012*).

- *First Serial Rights*: Rights given to a publication to publish the manuscript for the first time. Sometimes "North American" is added to these rights to provide a specific location of where the manuscript will be published.
- *One-time Rights*: Nonexclusive rights (means the work can be published with other publications, even simultaneously) purchased by a periodical to publish the work once.
- *Second Serial (Reprint) Rights*: Nonexclusive rights that allow a periodical to publish a manuscript after it has already been published elsewhere.
- *All Rights*: This means you are selling all possible rights to the publisher. You cannot use the article again.
- *Electronic Rights*: Rights for electronic media, including websites, CDs/DVDs, video games, smart phone apps, and more. The contract

should explain in more detail which forms of electronics it covers.

- *Subsidiary Rights*: Additional rights, other than for book publication, that need to be identified in the contract. This could be translation rights, various serial rights, and additional media or electronic rights, such as movie, television, audio, and others. Who has control of the rights, author or publisher, should be stated in the contract along with the percentage of sales that go to the author.
- *Dramatic, Television, and Motion Picture Rights*: Rights for using material on stage, on television, or in the movies.

Keep in mind: unspecified rights remain with the writer/author. Just be careful and aware of what rights you're signing over.

Write, Submit, and Get Paid

After signing the contract, it is time to write the article. Do research, get quotes, create an outline, and write a first draft. Then revise, edit, and proofread until your heart's content. Set it aside for a day or two and then return to it with a fresh outlook to edit some more.

When you're ready, you can submit the article to the editor. If they approve your article, you will either be paid on acceptance (when they confirm they want to publish your article and you agree) or on publication (after the article is published and printed). Payment on acceptance is better, since it can take months for an accepted article to be published.

As far as the payment they offer you, you can either take the offer they give you or try to get your article published elsewhere. However, after all of that work on querying your idea and tailoring the article to the publication, it is usually best to accept the offer, regardless of which payment type (on acceptance or on publication).

***

With the publishing industry, there is often a lot of waiting: waiting to hear back from editors, waiting for your articles to show up in the publication, waiting to be paid. It's the nature of the business. You must continue to write and continue to submit to magazines.

As you keep writing and publishing, the income will eventually becoming a steady stream.

Chapter 4
Ghostwriting

Ghostwriting is a commendable and higher-paying writing field. Ghostwriting, in essence, is getting paid for writing for someone and not having your byline (name) published with it, because they will use the piece of writing for their own purposes and may even claim it as theirs. The nature of the job is that you write for a professional who doesn't have the skills, time, or interest in a writing project and instead hires a ghostwriter by posting the job on an online job board or work-for-hire website.

Pros and Cons

Ghostwriting has its pros and cons. The pros are: higher pay, acknowledgement for your skills by the person who hires and pays you, fulfilling your love of writing, and helping someone. Ghostwriting can be a good way to break into publishing, as many new writers are nervous about publishing their writing—because they fear what people will think of it—so you will find out if you're a good writer, you will get paid, and you will get used to people reading (and accepting) your writing.

The cons of ghostwriting are: no name recognition and no rights to what you have written. Depending on your perspective of being a writer, ghostwriting may or may not be for you. But as a new writer in the freelance business, it's not a good idea to rule it out completely. Ghostwriting certainly can't hurt, and some people are solely ghostwriters.

Where Can You Find Ghostwriting Opportunities?

There are various websites that have ghostwriting opportunities: Textbroker, Elance, and oDesk to name a few. In addition, The Write Jobs and Craigslist sometimes advertise ghostwriting jobs along with their other writing jobs.

You can tell which posts are ghostwriting positions, because the job description will say: "I need help writing/editing/proofreading my book" or "I have the majority of my book completed, but I need help finishing it." Or they may come right out and say, "I need an article/book/webpage ghostwritten." They may even add, "All rights to the work revert to me and I will be publishing the work under my name/pseudonym."

The types of websites looking for ghostwriters are: job boards, work-for-hire (contracting) websites, and marketplaces for ghostwriting assignments.

Job Boards

Job boards post ghostwriting positions, and sometimes the employer does not explicitly state that it is a ghostwriting job, but you will be able to tell by the way the job description is worded. Job descriptions that say you will be doing writing for an individual are typically ghostwriting jobs, unless it says you will have a byline.

Work for Hire

Work-for-hire websites have contract positions that are usually temporary, in which you "bid" on a job and the client chooses one or more people to perform the job. These websites are highly competitive, like most open job positions, since multiple people apply for one job and usually only one gets hired. The slight twist is that when you bid on a job, you provide the client with a job proposal that includes: how qualified you are for the job, how much you charge, and how long it will take for you to complete the job. The client then has to decide on a qualified ghostwriter that they can afford and that can get the job done before its deadline, and the client usually doesn't provide details upfront about their budget or deadline. So it is really a shot in the dark. Also, the client might end up hiring no one, because they weren't satisfied with any of the job proposals they received.

However, the jobs you do get hired for will have lots of potential for earning substantial income, and gaining connections and future job opportunities.

Assignment Marketplaces

Certain websites are designed for writers to complete ghostwriting assignments and for clients to obtain quality writing at a good price. These marketplaces are listings of writing assignments that are posted by clients looking to pay someone to write for them. You simply search the assignments, and choose one that appeals to you and claim it. Then you write and edit the article and submit it to the client.

If and when the client approves your work, you get paid into your own account on the website. Once you earn over the withdrawal threshold, you can request payment at any time. As for Textbroker, the account balance must reach $10 or more, and you will typically receive payment in your PayPal account within a week.

These marketplaces provide great opportunities for freelance writers. Keep in mind that there are many writers scouting the assignments, and only one writer can claim an assignment, so be quick to claim one when you see one you like.

In addition, the number of assignments in the marketplace is determined by how and when clients post assignments. So, sometimes there are just a few available assignments to choose from, and sometimes there are hundreds. Be patient, claim wisely, write quickly, and you will have a profitable ghostwriting career.

Your Rate

When you begin ghostwriting, you will likely start at a rate of around one cent per word. It doesn't sound like much, but when you think about it, a 500-word article can earn you $5.00 and it only takes about an hour to write such an article. Not only are you making a little money, you are also gaining writing practice, confidence, and connections.

Experience, skills, and a good reputation will increase your rate on ghostwriting and work-for-hire websites that you participate in. If you regularly submit your best work—regardless of pay or the time it takes—you can acquire private clients and earn more income.

Private Clients

Ghostwriting for websites sometimes allows for special connections to occur where clients will want to hire you to do ghostwriting work outside the website. In addition, Twitter, Facebook, and LinkedIn are social networking websites where you can acquire private clients who will want to hire you for your ghostwriting services. Don't be afraid to make your freelance writing services known on these websites, and also in online writing forums, because you just may obtain private clients that way.

Chapter 5

Write a Book

Some freelance writers publish books or ebooks on the side as supplemental income and to get their name in the public eye. A book is a means of marketing your writing services and a form of income.

It takes interest, dedication, time, and patience to complete a book project. Let's review why.

Interest

Interest is the first thing you will encounter as you brainstorm book ideas. You will become interested in a topic or storyline. You might ponder it in your mind for days. You will then begin writing about it.

This initial interest must be maintained in order to write about your topic or storyline for consecutive months or years. Therefore, pick a topic that you have lots to say about or a storyline that really excites you. You should create an outline in the beginning, whether your book is fiction or nonfiction. Getting your ideas down while they are flowing will leave you with ideas to spark your interest during times when you feel like your ideas are limited.

As you move along in the writing process, periodically remind yourself of your great interest in your book that was there in the beginning. Your interest might start to fade, so you will have to fan the fire, so to speak, to keep your interest strong. Your interest must continue in order to finish writing, editing, and publishing your book. If you lose interest, you might not complete the process. Writing daily, being dedicated to the process and your topic, and reminding yourself of your initial interest will help keep your interest in your book alive in order to complete the project.

Dedication

It's often easy to start a book, because you're all revved up with a great idea and you're aching to write it down. But it's another thing to complete the entire book creation process. Getting through the first draft is hard, and editing several times is draining and makes the project seem impossible to get through.

It helps to talk to people about your book project, whether in person, online, or both. Telling others how excited you are about your project and book topic will make the idea more real in your mind. It will also hold you accountable to doing what you say you will do (write a book!).

You will need to be dedicated to your book project or else it won't get finished. You need to find, inside yourself, the desire to dedicate your efforts to writing and completing your book. You can do this by reminding yourself daily of your initial interest in your book, and writing daily until the first draft is complete. Then wait a couple of weeks to edit and in between edits. Hold tight to your feeling of dedication and your book *will* get done.

Time

Writing a book is time-consuming, for it takes months to years to write a book. The exact time depends on the length of the book, how much time in a day you spend working on it, the effort you put into the quality of your writing, if the book comes together easily or takes a lot of effort to write, how much time you spend editing and formatting the book, and if you traditionally publish or self-publish.

Books can be twenty pages to one-thousand pages, so the number of pages definitely affects how long it will take to write the book. How much time each day or each week you dedicate to writing the book has a direct impact on how many months or years it will take to complete it.

Books can turn out anywhere from sloppy to pristine. A book that was quickly typed and had little or no editing, will be finished sooner than a book in which the author spent significant time during the writing, editing, and formatting processes.

Some books come together easily, coming out of the author and going onto paper effortlessly. While some books—actually, most books—take more effort and struggle for the author to convey what they want to say and how they want to say it, and for the chapters to come together cohesively.

The initial composure of a book affects the editing process, since a book that is easy to write usually takes less writing and editing time than a book in which the writing is like "pulling teeth." Additionally, the amount of time spent on each stage of the book's creation process, can indirectly affect the amount of time a book takes to finish. For example, a writer who puts more effort into the first draft (which sometimes equals more time, depending on if the book comes together easily or difficultly), might have less revising to do, which *could* affect the total time.

Self-publishing can take one day or several days to complete the publishing process. With traditional publishing the publishing process can take months, because you must first query agents, then be accepted by a publisher, and then go through the editing, formatting, and publication processes.

Patience

Because of the time writing and publishing a book requires, patience is essential. You will need to exhibit patience while you write, edit, and format your book. You will need to be patient during all the stages of the book creation process, so that you will create a product worthy of your time spent on it and readers' time reading it. You will want to create a polished product or else it won't sell. Have respect for yourself and others by taking the time to create a well-made book.

You must also possess patience during the publishing process. If you wish to traditionally publish, your time will be spent waiting for publication to happen on the publisher's end, and you will need to remain patient. If you decide to self-publish, it takes time to acquire a cover design—whether you create your own or hire someone to do it; format the documents, because each epublisher has different formatting requirements; and during the last steps it takes time to enter the book's and author's information, upload the book's interior and exterior files, and make sure everything is correct before clicking the "publish" button. All of the time that is required to publish asks for your patience, but is well worth the wait.

***

One of the first things you should decide before writing your book is what format it will be. Do you want to publish a print book, an ebook, or both? There are differences between them as far as cost and format.

Print Books

If you want a hard copy of your book or want to have a book signing, you will probably want your book in print. Print books are the most expensive book type and have a standard format.

Cost of Print Books

Mass market paperbacks cost anywhere from $5 to $10. Children's books and picture books usually cost $5 to $20. Print books that are fiction or nonfiction typically cost $10 to $25, depending on if the book is a paperback or hardcover. Textbooks and professional books cost about $25 to $125.

Format of Print Books

Most book covers have color and graphics. The back cover usually includes a synopsis and author biography. There are different types of bindings available, such as perfect binding (for most hardcovers and paperbacks), saddle stitching (stapled through the middle), or spiral, loop, or coil binding.

Fiction and nonfiction books, including mass market paperbacks, are mostly black and white on the inside with the majority being plain text. Most have parts and/or chapters, and some have headings in bold font. Sometimes, but rarely, there are images.

Children's books are more likely to have images, especially picture books which have the most images—many in color.

Professional books are mostly black and white on the inside, but have charts and diagrams to educate the professional. Textbooks are more apt to have images in color.

Ebooks

If you are interested in publishing a book quickly and inexpensively, ebooks are a good solution. Ebooks are technically "electronic books." You can read them on a computer or an e-reader device. Ebooks have risen in popularity over the last several years and are similar to the relationship between computers and paper and pen. Because computers are so prevalent today, it is wise to learn about ebooks, or even try publishing one.

Cost of Ebooks

Because there are no printing costs and no manufacturing process, ebooks are less expensive to create and are, therefore, less costly to readers. Writers earn a larger percentage of the profits. Everyone likes the savings and cheapness of an ebook. In fact, some authors offer their ebooks for free as a marketing tool (writing for free will be covered in the next chapter).

Generally speaking, ebooks range in price from $1 to $15, with most being under $10. In fact, certain e-publishers will not allow authors to charge more than $10 for an ebook, in order to get more sales, and in turn, more profits.

Format of Ebooks

Being an electronic book, an ebook is formatted to look and function more like a webpage. This is because people who read documents on the Internet tend to "scan" them (look for the information they need quickly) and move on to the next page (if they are disinterested or cannot immediately find the information they need) quicker than when reading a print publication. If the reader or prospective customer "moves on," the author could lose a reader or a sale. So to help the potential buyer or reader find the information they need (and hopefully encourage their interest), many ebook authors use bold headings, images, and lists in their ebooks.

Publishing a Book as Both a Print Book and an Ebook

If you wish to publish your book as both a print book and an ebook, it is wise to create and publish the print book first, and then add formatting, white space, and images (if you wish) to the document, and save it as a different file in order to save both copies of the book. Spending the extra time to tailor your book to both print and electronic mediums is a wise and profitable endeavor.

Traditional Publishing Process

Publishing a book the traditional way is similar to the process of submitting an article to a print publication. Nonfiction and fiction are handled differently.

Publishing Nonfiction Books Traditionally

If you want to traditionally publish a nonfiction book, you will need to find a literary agent or a publisher. A literary agent will propose your book idea to publishers, support you in your writing career, and try to get you a better publishing deal. Or you can go directly to a publisher. But keep in mind that most publishers take on authors who are represented by agents, especially new authors, and some publishers do not even look at unsolicited material from writers.

What you can do is look up publishers on their websites, or in *Writer's Market*, to determine if they accept new author submissions. If they do, find out their submission guidelines on their website, in *Writer's Market*, by emailing or calling them, or by sending them a letter requesting a copy of their submission guidelines.

Most agents and publishers accept submissions for nonfiction books that haven't been completed yet. So if you have a great idea and know that you will be able to successfully write and finish the book, you can query the agent or publisher before you have finished the book. However, if you prefer to write the entire book before pursuing an agent or publisher, there is no harm done, because you can always self-publish if you cannot get traditionally published. Writing is never a waste.

Now that you have the submission guidelines, and you know the agent or publisher is accepting new writers, your next step is to query them. Querying consists of sending one or more of the following documents to an agent or publisher:

- Query letter (typically includes a book description followed by an author biography)
- Marketing and promoting plan
- Competitive titles already published on the topic (and how your book is different)
- Chapter outline
- Sample pages or chapters

It is fine to query more than one publisher or agent, but make sure to keep track of who you queried and when. Emailing is usually the preferred choice for submissions, which is easier for both you and the agent or publisher. Most agents and publishers do not open email attachments, so read the submission guidelines carefully to determine if this is the case with the one you've chosen. Along those lines, follow the submission guidelines *exactly*. This is very important, because it reflects intelligence, professionalism, and cooperation on your part.

Publishing Fiction Books Traditionally

If you plan on publishing a work of fiction, you definitely will need a literary agent. Publishers typically do not accept unsolicited fiction material. You can find a literary agent through a Web search, *Writer's Market* book or website, and Preditors & Editors website. On Preditors & Editors, you can see if the agent is "recommended" or at least doesn't have any negative feedback from clients.

Before submitting anything to an agent, your novel must be complete and polished. If it is not, the agent won't represent you. Finish writing the rest of the novel—all the way to the end—and then read through it and revise, edit, and proofread at least once, but preferably two or three times. Once you feel you have an excellent novel that is free of most errors, you can select a few agents to query.

Like with nonfiction works, you will need to look up the submission guidelines on the agents' websites for each agent you have chosen and, preferably, develop separate submissions for each, because each agent will want a slightly different type of submission. You will have a much better chance of getting an agent if your submission is tailored to their requirements.

Your query package should consist of one or more of the following:

- Query letter (typically includes a synopsis and an author biography)
- A sample of the manuscript (no more than the first 50 pages or a few sample chapters either consecutively or inconsecutively, depending on the submission guidelines)

  (OR)
- The entire manuscript (rare for unsolicited)

It is very important to format your manuscript according to the agent's preference. If they do not supply formatting details, this standard format applies: heading, followed by centered book title on first page, followed by manuscript; page numbers on each page; double spaced; Times New Roman or Arial in size 10 or 12-point; and one-inch margins.

As with nonfiction, you can query more than one agent. If you are submitting your entire manuscript, because it was requested in the submission guidelines, or the agent or publisher requested it, your best bet is to mail it in a small, secured box to preserve the pages, unless the agent prefers it to be emailed and will open the attachment. Depending on the number of pages of your document, you may not be able to upload it as an attachment because your email program may not support the file size. So in that case, you will have to mail it.

As with nonfiction, you have the option of self-publishing, or publishing with a print-on-demand company, if you cannot obtain an agent in a reasonable amount of time, which is determined by your level of patience and tolerance.

Self-Publishing

Self-publishing a book is usually done with a small press or on the Internet as an ebook. The press method is for creating print books and is viable for writers who have money to invest in publishing their book, for those who want to obtain their books in bulk quantities, and for those who want to keep all the profits from their book sales. Many self-published writers must hire a team to help them with editing, cover design, sales and distribution, and marketing. Some, however, do the entire process themselves, which saves money, but is time-consuming and hard work.

The other method—creating an ebook—is free to produce, you receive a large percentage of the profits, and there are no shipping or handling charges or manufacturing costs. You still need to promote and market your book (or hire someone to do it for you), but that is the same with traditional publishing and the press method of self-publishing.

Ebooks come in various formats. Some of the more common ones are: kindle (mobi), nook (epub), and PDF. *Kindle Direct Publishing* (Amazon) and

Smashwords are the two most popular e-publishers, because creating an ebook with either of them costs nothing, and *Amazon* is widely known and used often as a book retailer and *Smashwords* distributes to numerous popular retailers at once.

Print-on-Demand Publishing

Print-on-demand (POD) publishing means that print books are manufactured and shipped to order. The books are printed based on each customer's order, whether it is for one book or one-hundred copies of the same book. Every time there is a new order, the order is filled and shipped.

POD companies handle many authors at once. Therefore, they fill numerous orders as the orders are placed by the authors and customers. POD companies get a share of the book's cost for labor and materials from manufacturing and producing the copies, and a small percentage of the profits for commission.

POD companies have websites where you can create your books from scratch by choosing book size and shape, type of paper, binding, book style (hardcover, paperback, stapled), and uploading your cover design, back cover, and interior files. Then you must order a proof copy, review it, and approve it for distribution. Afterwards, your book will be available for customers to purchase.

Some companies, such as *Lulu*, do "open publishing," which is essentially a company that allows you to create, order, and distribute your book in *both* print and ebook formats.

A Final Word

It is important to spend time writing, revising, formatting, uploading, and designing your book. Creating a book is a lengthy process, but the book will be around forever, so take your time with it. Quality is the difference between a best seller and a book that doesn't sell. Your book is like a baby, so spend a lot of time taking care of it before releasing it to the world where it will be on its own. Additionally, you have one chance to make a good first impression with your book, so be patient with the process and you will unveil a beautiful gem that everyone will enjoy.

Chapter 6

Write for Free

You must be thinking: "Write for free? Are you crazy? How am I going to get *anywhere* writing for free?" Believe it or not, there are many reasons why freelance writers write for free.

Actually, you probably write for free already: emails, blog posts, forum posts, status updates, and tweets—to name a few. Or even, letters and cards. When you do so, you make yourself known to the world. You make your words, message, and name visible to others. This is called creating a brand for yourself. You are developing a writing identity.

As a freelance writer, your brand is important. Readers will associate your name with your style of writing. If you wish to keep your writing identity separate from your real identity, or if you simply wish to remain anonymous, you can use a pen name.

Your brand is something you market, and it is part of developing a readership. Writing for free encourages readers to get to know you. Eventually, they may decide to pay for your services. In addition, you can market yourself within your "free" writing to obtain *paid* writing assignments by including links to your website and articles.

There are three main purposes that writing-for-free serves: marketing, gaining readership, and indirect income.

Marketing

The purpose of marketing is to make your name, your writing, and your writing style known. Marketing is the same as saying, "Hey, I'm right here! Come check out my writing!" You'll want to establish your niche in the writing world. That is not the same as choosing a genre to write about and sticking to it. Rather, you do *not* need to create a label for yourself as a writer. Your brand or niche is your writing style, voice, message—that which makes you unique as a writer.

You may decide that you want to be known under a certain genre. Or you may decide that you like variety and want to share your knowledge about a variety of topics. Either is perfectly fine. Which one you choose depends only on what you prefer as a writer. Or you may choose to make *no* choice and instead just go with the flow. That, too, is okay.

There are several ways to market yourself and your writing by writing for free. You can publish articles on websites, such as EzineArticles and Squidoo, where people go for information. Readers will see your writer biography, and if they like your work, they may decide to look into other pieces you've published or your website.

You can start a blog (it's best to have a central theme, goal, or purpose in mind) and publish posts weekly or daily. On the "about me" page, you can provide information about yourself, your writing, and your brand.

You can also write a short ebook and offer it to readers for signing up for your website's newsletter, for following or joining your blog, or as a way to gain their attention so that they will check out your other writing pieces.

Gaining Readership

Everyone likes things that are free. By offering free writing, you will attract readers and, eventually, a following of fans. If you have published articles, you will gain readers who may look into reading your other articles. This is especially true if they like your writing style. If you have a blog, people will read it and some of them might follow or join it, or become a fan. The more often you publish for free, the more your writing will be visible, and the larger your readership will be.

Readers are necessary for writers to prosper. By publishing your writing, you are allowing people to read what you've written, and if it's quality writing, they will come back for more. Having readers will also lead to improving your writing, as you will receive suggestions and feedback. Don't be afraid to publish because people will read what you wrote. But when you do publish, make sure it's quality.

Indirect Income

Free writing leads to making money. "How?" you ask. Because free writing encourages people to read your writing that pays or hire you for a writing project, and you can put an author biography and links to your paid writing within the free writing. The information and links will allow the reader to learn more about you if they like what they have seen of your writing so far. That is why quality writing is so important.

Here are some examples of how you can earn money from free writing:

- You publish an article that links to your author biography where you have your freelance writing website listed, which is where you can be contacted for paid writing services.
- You publish a blog post and the "about me" page has a link to a book you've written that is for sale.

- You publish a short ebook that has links throughout to your various articles that you get paid for from a combination of revenue share and page views (covered in chapter 21).

In those instances, you can earn money when the readers are interested enough to click through to learn more about you. So give them a reason to do so!

PART 2

MARKETING

Chapter 7
Forms of Marketing

Marketing is a business tactic that not only lets people know the business exists, but also keeps the business running smoothly and increases the customer base. As a freelance writer, you are running a business. Therefore, you will need to use marketing techniques.

As a freelance writer, marketing is necessary to let people know about your writing, whether it is published online or in print. There are different ways to market: advertising materials, social networking websites, online communities, and in person.

Advertising Materials

Advertising materials are items that can be used to promote your business, such as business cards, postcards, pens, and bookmarks—with your business labeled on them. Depending on the size of the item, you can include various bits of information about your writing business. The goal is to always have the advertising material lead the potential customer to your website, blog, phone, or email. By including your website's URL, or your email address, along with a promotional message, there is a "call to action" that includes a way for the customer to learn more about your writing and your services.

Use the advertising space wisely, but do not clutter the material. A clear, concise, to-the-point advertisement will spark the reader's interest and hold their attention long enough for them to consider contacting you. They might visit your website, or email you for writing services.

For the advertising part, it is good to use some, or all, of the following information: your name as a bold heading, your title (freelance writer) underneath, one sentence or phrase that describes you as a writer (or your writing style), the writing services you offer, your website or blog, and your email address.

Pens are small, so you'll have to be brief with your advertisement: use the most important information, such as your name, your website, and a catch-phrase. Or you can simply put your name, title, and website on the pen and give them away as a promotional gift to customers you already have or potential ones you meet.

There are endless things you can advertise as a writer; here are just a few ideas: books, blogs, articles, poetry, professional services, websites. Anything writing related, that you want people to take a look at, is worth advertising.

Paper items (business cards, postcards, bookmarks) can be created and ordered online from websites like Moo and VistaPrint. Moo is more expensive per item, they sell smaller quantities, and their products are high quality. If you aren't looking for a large quantity of the same item, the order could cost the same or less. And you can have multiple images in each order. VistaPrint is similar, but they are less expensive and make large quantities, which can be very helpful if you know a lot of people to share your advertising materials with, or if you have a marketing plan and it would require hundreds of copies. They also have a lot of freebies. Which company you choose to use for your advertising materials depends on your business' needs.

Social Networking Websites

Facebook, Twitter, and LinkedIn are websites that are social in nature where you can get involved and share your brand and services. A rule of thumb is to not bombard your connections with advertising, because eventually they will stop listening to you and may even block you. The best thing to do is to gradually add connections while you establish your brand. Then begin to post occasional links to your writing, along with other types of posts, while also checking out your connections' writings in return.

Each social networking website works slightly different. Facebook is more casual and friendly, but also has professional pages. Twitter is similar to a very short press release that you submit to all of your followers. LinkedIn is for anyone that has held a job to have a profile with their resume information, interact in groups that interest them, and connect to other workers and employers.

On these social networking sites, you can type one sentence and send the message to hundreds (or thousands) of your connections. There are even websites, such as HootSuite, that are a central location for all of your social networking profiles, and you can send your message to all of the sites at once in order to be more efficient if you have many social network accounts.

Social networking websites are a quick way to broadcast information to lots of people. If used reasonably, they can be a very useful tool.

Online Communities

Online writing and reading communities give you the opportunity to share your writing with a close-knit group. You can do a search for online forums based on your interests as well. Writer's Digest Community has an online forum, a blog, and groups for writers. Goodreads is a community of authors and readers, where authors market their books and readers post book reviews. Those are just two examples, but there are plenty of more communities depending on what you're interested in. For example, if you like to write about science, you can share and market your science writing on science forums.

Being that online communities revolve around a central theme, their population is typically less than the total on social networking websites, so you need to be softer with advertising or else you could be considered a spammer and banned from the community. Online communities are more for getting to know other people in the world that share similar interests in order to increase your network (more about networking in chapter 9).

Once you have established camaraderie amongst the members of the community, you can share some things about you, such as your blog posts, information about writing you've published, and links to your writing (if it will help someone else). Online forums offer a more subtle way to advertise, but all advertising helps.

In Person

Even though most of a freelance writing business is done online, you will still likely go out and see people. And that is a good opportunity to share the nature of your business. The conversations don't have to be just with people you know. You should also reach out and meet new people to obtain new customers.

Being friendly to a person who appears nice can lead to a business deal. Strike up a conversation with someone in line with you at a store register. Make a friendly comment, smile, tell them a little about yourself, exchange a few words, and give him or her a few of your business cards or a bookmark. They will surely appreciate the gesture. Plus, you will become more comfortable marketing yourself as a self-employed business person.

All businesses must interact with customers, and some of the interaction ends up being in person. Take the initiative to make an exchange with new people, and gain new connections in the process.

Concluding Words of Advice

As a freelance writer you'll need to get used to promoting yourself, marketing your business, and connecting with people. Don't be afraid or shy when you make yourself known. It takes a little practice to get used to talking about your skills and your work.

Don't think of it as bragging or rude. Think of it as: you are the owner of your business and you have a product to sell, so you will honestly and positively inform people about it. It can be hard at first, but the more you do it, the easier it will get. In fact, one day you just may enjoy marketing and promotion!

Chapter 8

Manage a Website, Blog, or Both!

As a freelance writer in the 21st century, you will need a website, blog, or both. There are free ways to have a website or blog, so there is no reason not to. Generally speaking, websites are a way to market your product (your writing, or yourself—as a freelance writer). Blogs are a way to connect—share your thoughts and knowledge—with your readers. You can also have a website that has a blog as one of its pages if you prefer to be efficient. Let's review aspects about websites and blogs separately.

Websites

A website is like a large advertisement for a product or service. You will need one if you are going to be a freelance writer. There are different ways that you can set up your website, as far as the approach and features you use.

Home Page

A freelance writer's website needs to catch visitors' attentions on the very first page, also called the home page. On the home page, you should provide concise and direct statements about yourself and your services. Keep your future visitors in mind while you design it. In other words, pretend you are a visitor when you create your home page, and design and compose it in a way that would attract your attention and make you want to look into the website more.

Change the formatting depending on what best communicates the message you intend to give. It's a good rule of thumb to make the most important words bold and the headings larger in size than the text below them. Use images, or preferably, develop a trademark image for your freelance writing business and put it on the home page. You can also upload a picture of yourself if you wish. But keep your home page simple. Too many images or different fonts can detract the visitors' attentions away from your business purpose and also your website.

Other Pages

Other pages you can include on your website are: resume, services, writing samples, and links to your published writing. Include any other information or pages that will represent you as a professional freelance writer. Also, leave unnecessary information off your website. Less is more.

Additional Tips

Make sure your resume is current, your links are working correctly, and the information is accurate on every page. Keep your website updated, and add new information periodically to ensure more traffic to your website.

Also make sure you are communicating the image you wish you portray. View your website through your visitors' minds, so to speak. And don't be afraid to "strut your stuff." If you are a good writer, tell the world what makes you good. If you have additional skills and qualities—related to your writing career—include them.

Blogs

Blogs are similar to websites, but they also have their differences. Blogs are more conversational, and therefore, considered as a more casual location for publishing. However, some websites are very casual, and some blogs are very professional, so it can go both ways. But, generally speaking, a blog is a collection of chronological posts that the blog owner makes individually, and visitors to the blog can read and comment on the posts.

A blog post typically communicates one main idea and provides details related to that idea. Blog posts are ideally short (300-500 words), so the writer needs to be concise with their message. This is done by using short words, sentences that are direct, and action verbs that speak to and draw in the readers.

Blogs are good marketing tools because you can have an "about me" page on them, where you can provide information about yourself as a writer or your writing business. You can provide links to your online writing profiles, so that visitors to your blog can check out other writing you've done. They will be more likely to do this if they like the writing style you've reflected in your blog posts. Therefore, it is commendable to publish your best writing in blog posts. People want to learn more about other people who communicate effectively, so if you do so in your blog posts, you will have more business.

Like websites, blogs should be updated regularly. The most successful blogs are ones where there are new posts at least every week (preferably every day). By posting on a regular basis you are giving your visitors, and especially your regular followers, exactly what they seek—interesting information from an interesting writer. The more often you post, the more followers and blog hits you'll get.

***

Blogs and websites can be used to promote your writing services and published writing. Blogs can be a good way to interact with your readers on a more personal level, which also leads to having more readers.

Websites allow you to sell yourself as a professional writer. People searching the Web for freelance writers will find your website (more on search engine optimization in chapter 16), and if they become interested in you, they will contact you through your website. If you do not wish to have private clients, you can provide links to your published writing to earn money on the page views (more about getting paid in chapter 21).

Blogs and websites both have the ability to have advertisements on them and earn income from the ads. Check out (online) Google AdSense to learn more about earning money from content and user-related ads on your website or blog, Google Affiliate for earning money from advertised products, and Amazon Associates for earning money from advertised Amazon.com products (more about getting paid through advertising in chapter 21).

All in all, blogs and websites are effective marketing tools that connect you to your readers and customers. Don't abuse their marketing abilities—by using too many advertisements or big, flashy ads—or it could end up hindering your efforts. Instead, use ads moderately and wisely, and your viewers will thank you.

Chapter 9

Networking

Networking is very important for freelance writers. In order to run a writing business, you will need to network with others. As an example: a famous writer doesn't become famous alone; she has lots of fans that help her reach her fame. And she helps them in return with her powerful messages and stories.

Start Small

Begin by writing and being you. Discover what you like to write and get good at it by practicing. It takes a long time to become a good writer, and the only way you will get there is if you write, learn, and repeat.

Once you have developed your craft and think you might be good at writing, publish some of your writing.

See how your readers react. Respond to their comments. Be polite and friendly. Gain readers of your work.

Next, comment on *their* writing. Look for other writers that you can encourage. Share what you know. Build a network of connections and readers.

All the while, expand your network. Look for publishers and editors, and get to know them. Write to them and maybe they'll write you back. In fact, they probably will.

In order for people to read your writing, you need to know people and let them know that you've written something. People will spread the word to other people and your readership will grow.

That is how ordinary writers gain readers of their work and clients. Rarely will an unknown writer become famous overnight, so you must work hard at developing a readership. But that's all part of the journey to doing what you love.

Interviewing

Writers and authors can interview each other on their blogs. A writer who wants to publish more blog posts and grow their readership figures that interviewing another writer (or author) would be a good way to do so. Because the interviewed writer gains exposure, the deed is good for both of them. As a freelance writer who has a blog, you could be either the interviewer or the interviewee.

Online Forums

Writer forums, and all other types of forums that interest you, are good places to join and network with likeminded individuals. Share your knowledge, post discussions, and ask questions. Online forums are full of helpful information, a chance to network with people like you, and a place to advertise and gain readership as well (you can post links in forums—either on your profile page or in your discussion posts—to your articles, poetry, books, blogs, websites, etc.).

Gain Connections

Networking allows you to help others, and allows others to help you—to succeed. It's a win-win situation. Everyone will rise to the top together.

On your way to the top, networking allows you to meet other writers, authors, editors, agents, and publishers. You can learn from each other and help each other. One person has a lot to give, and in return you will likely get back much more than you give.

Chapter 10
Electronic Signatures

A signature is a short quote of your own professional information that you want everyone to know. When used at the end of a message, it is helpful for a professional appearance and for others to connect with you better.

Professional Email Address

It is best to have a professional email address for all business correspondence. If you have or plan on having a website, it is a good idea to apply for a domain name that has a matching email address. Make the domain name professional by including keywords or your name. For the email address, use your first name before the "@" sign, which will be followed by the website's domain name. Using a professional email address will help when corresponding with clients and potential clients.

Creating a Signature

Whichever email program you use, there will be the option to add a signature. An email signature provides information that identifies you and your profession, and gives people the information in which you can be contacted.

In order to add a signature, type in the information that you want to appear at the bottom of every business email, such as your name, title, and website. Save it so that you will be able to add your signature to any email you wish by clicking an "insert signature" button where you want your signature in the email.

If you will be using the email account for business purposes only, it will be a good idea to program the signature to show up automatically for every email. You can do this through the "options" category in your email program. Even when the signature is added automatically, it can still be deleted like any typed text, so don't worry if you think there may be occasions when you might not want it to be included in your email message.

Functionality in Emails

Providing your contact information via a signature allows others to contact you based on your preferred method. This is convenient for both you and your contacts. Yes, they can just reply to your email to reach you. But what if they want to learn more about you? Your title, the name of your business, and your website URL will be available to them instantaneously. Help them find out more about you easily by providing this key information at the end of your emails.

Signatures in Forums

Some forums allow members to create signatures that will appear at the bottom of every message they post. If the forum you participate in has that option, definitely use it. But keep the amount of information brief. Putting a concise, convincing sentence with an inserted hyperlink for your blog or website is sufficient.

Creating Hyperlinks

A hyperlink is a link hidden by words. Hyperlinks are a quick and effective way to encourage someone to go somewhere on the Web that you want them to go. The proper way to use a hyperlink is to create it within the appropriate words. For example, with the sentence: "Check out my website!" *website* or *my website* would have the website's link embedded in it.

Most of the time, in text boxes online, there is the ability to insert a hyperlink into the text box by clicking on a button above the text box. That is the preferred method, for most people, for creating a hyperlink.

A hyperlink can also be created manually by using the following HTML code within your post:

<a href="link">my website</a>

You would need to replace **link** with the URL (but keep the quotation marks around the link) and **my website** is the text that will display to others.

Importance of Quality Writing

Every time someone reads your forum posts or emails they will see your signature and may click on your website's link. Therefore, you will need to make sure all of your posts and emails are written with quality, as if you are publishing them, because in actuality you are! Everything posted on the web is published, because other people are free to read it. It's important to have quality forum posts and emails, so that viewers and contacts will be compelled to find out more about you.

PART 3

JOBS AND JOB SEARCHING

Chapter 11

Searching for Writing Jobs

Freelance writing jobs, whether they involve ghostwriting, resume writing, blog posting, book reviews, or whatever interests you, are a part of being a freelance writing career if you so choose. Often, they can be higher on the pay scale. Usually they are found on work-for-hire websites, job boards, or directly at the businesses' websites. Read on to learn more about the ways to obtain a writing job.

Importance of Education When Obtaining a Job

First of all, since education is related to job searching, because it appears on your resume and companies will ask you about it, let's review the importance of having an education.

A college education will help you when you apply for writing jobs, because it will automatically make you more qualified than a candidate who has the same work history or experience as you but doesn't have college experience. And the closer your educational degree or certificate relates to the job description, the more qualified you will appear to the company you apply to or who seeks you out.

It is very admirable to have an advanced education. School takes a lot of hard work, time, and dedication as well as perseverance to accomplish the degree or certificate. If you have a college education, you should be very proud of your accomplishments.

For those who don't have an advanced education, you have the ability to climb the corporate ladder, so to speak. This is because life itself is an education, as you probably already know, and you can learn a lot of valuable information and skills from your experiences. You too should be proud of your accomplishments.

You also have the ability to return to school now or at any time, if you so choose. It is never too late to obtain a college education. It only takes the drive to succeed.

Reading this book shows you are ambitious and bright, since you are contemplating taking the next steps to becoming a freelance writer and are researching your options.

The Significance of Writing Jobs

The next step of freelance writing that you should consider are applying for writing jobs. You don't have to obtain a writing job to be a freelance writer, but it is something to think about. Generally speaking, a writing job is more concrete and provides significant income, compared to writing for content websites for example.

If obtaining a writing job is your goal, then this chapter is for you. If you want to stick with writing articles, blog posts, and books, that's great too. You can learn something new about writing in this chapter, so stick around. This chapter will provide information specific to searching for writing jobs, and also information that can be applied when searching for any job.

There are various ways to search for a writing job, but the four main methods are: online, in print, in person, and by word-of-mouth.

Search Online for Writing Jobs

Searching online is the most common way to find a job these days, as almost everything can be found and done online. There are general job searching websites like Monster, CareerBuilder, and Indeed where you can find freelance writing jobs, and industry specific job databases like Journalism Jobs and The Write Jobs. The Telecommute Job List also has freelance writing jobs. Many freelance writing websites, such as Freelance Writing and About Freelance Writing, have job listings. You can also search for freelance writing jobs on professional networking websites like LinkedIn.

How to Search Online Databases Correctly

The technical aspect of searching online for writing jobs involves knowing how to use the search tools to find jobs that you'd be interested in. If you have your mind set on a job title that is very specific, simply type the job title into the keyword search bar and click "enter." Otherwise, you can go to the "advanced search" page to have more control over your search results.

On the advanced search page, you'll want to determine the characteristics of a writing job that are most important to you. As an example, the main characteristic might be the ability to telecommute, as that is what most freelance writers want to do. Even with a telecommuting position, you might pick a location, such as your state or city, in case the company will want to meet you in person.

You might also have a writing niche in mind, such as resume writing, copy writing, or editing, which you can type in the "keywords" section. Lastly, you might want to organize your search results by selecting a date range or choosing to list the results according to the posting date.

Once you have entered the information you want included in the search results, click "search." By doing that, you will have created a unique search of all the job listings. If you did not get enough results to your liking, you can expand the search results by using less search criteria. Play around with it until you find the best search criteria and method for your needs.

Search Print Ads for Writing Jobs

Newspapers and magazines are additional ways to find freelance writing jobs. The selection of jobs is, in fact, different in print than online. So, check the classifieds in newspapers and periodicals. You can do this by subscribing to your local or regional newspaper or by buying a Sunday paper in a convenience store each week.

Look through all the classifieds, circling the writing jobs that appeal to you. Then, go back through just the ones that interested you and type up a list of the job listings, including the specifics. Then, one by one, you can call, email, or visit the website of each contact and apply for the positions. Keep notes of your communications and include dates. Continue to follow up each week until you get the position or are told the position is no longer available.

Search for a Writing Job in Person

You can also search for jobs when you go places by car or by foot (if you live in the city). Some businesses advertise in their establishments when they need to fill a job position. You can also inquire at reception desks and leave your business card. Job opportunities are everywhere; you just have to look.

Search for a Writing Job by Word of Mouth

Obtaining a writing job by word of mouth involves networking, usually on the phone. All the socializing you do on a daily basis can actually help you obtain a job. Talk to people you know—friends, family, coworkers, and prior connections—and ask them if they know anyone who is looking for a writer. There is a large potential for positive responses, and you won't know until you ask. So ask!

Job Search Process

There is a standard process, when working on obtaining a job, that everyone should know. It begins with searching for a job—which has already been covered. Next is to apply for the job.

Applying for the Job

Once you find a job you're interested in, you'll want to apply to it. This can be done through an online application, print application, or email. When you apply, you'll definitely want to provide the company with as much information about yourself as possible so that they will be able to fairly evaluate you as a candidate. Don't be afraid to include your accomplishments, experience, awards, and education—to give yourself a fair chance at obtaining the job. Remember, the job market is very competitive.

Following up on Your Application

After you apply for the job, if the manager's contact information is available, follow up within one week (if you haven't been contacted by them) to make sure your application was received, and to let them know you are very interested in the job. Following up can seal a deal, so to speak, so it is very worthwhile to do. Some companies may disregard your application if you do not follow up, because they have an overwhelming number of applicants. Continue to follow-up every week as long as the position remains open.

The Interview

If the company calls you to set up an interview, you will need to prepare for it. If the interview will be in person, pick out a conservative outfit that is clean; review your resume; think about what you want to say in the interview; and print out an online map of where the interview will be held, or even drive to the location prior to the interview. In the interview, be polite, feel confident, and show your professionalism. Answer the interviewer's questions directly and completely. Smile, and help yourself to feel as comfortable as possible by thinking positive affirmations.

If the interview is over the phone, plan out what you will say, and write down some notes so that you don't forget anything. Smile while you talk on the phone during the interview, as it will reflect a pleasant, upbeat, and friendly voice.

If you have questions about the position, ask them at the end of the interview or when the interviewer asks you if you have any questions. Thank the interviewer for their time and restate your interest in the position with enthusiasm.

After the Interview

After the interview you should send the interviewer a thank you note—either by email or postal mail. Follow up with a phone call in one week, if you haven't heard from them, to politely remind them that you had an interview and would like to know if they have made a decision about the job position yet. One or two follow ups is enough. You don't want to appear pushy and you don't want to burn any bridges by overstepping boundaries.

***

It often takes a long time to obtain a writing job, but if you keep trying and don't get discouraged, eventually you will. So stand strong and keep persevering.

Chapter 12
Crafting a Resume

Resumes are your ticket to a writing job or a client connection. Resumes are like a detailed business card that has additional information, such as your education and work history. Before you hand out your resume, make sure it is most effective by being current.

The Importance of Keeping Your Resume Updated

It is important for every worker to keep an updated resume in their files. A resume is a record of your work history, education, skills, and milestones. The more often you update your resume, the easier it is to maintain. At the very least, it is important to save your dates of employment (month and year) for every position, your past employers' contact information, and the skills you learned, so that you don't forget them!

Keeping an updated resume is beneficial. If you do so, and if you are interested in a writing position, you won't have to spend hours or days collecting the information to make your resume current and in good condition to submit.

If your resume information is not current, the potential employer might think you have gaps in your employment history, which will hurt your chance of getting the job. You also want to make sure to include all of your skills, to help your chance of getting the position, which cannot be done if your resume is outdated. Also, your resume's objective section will not likely match the job you are interested in if you submit an old resume. Overall, you will *not* be representing yourself in the best way possible.

The best way to keep a resume current is to update it every year or whenever there are changes in your employment or education. For the most part, only the most recent information will need to be added or updated. That is, unless you wish to redo your resume's style, or if the work history is over ten years old (more about that later in this chapter), so it is pretty painless.

It is reassuring when you see a writing position you may be interested in and your resume is nearly ready to submit, rather than if you need to overhaul your resume, or even worse—write one from scratch. An updated resume also makes job hunting less stressful and overwhelming.

Post Your Resume Online

If you have a website for your writing career and you want to attract business and clients, post a copy of your resume on it. You can include as much or as little information that you feel comfortable sharing online. You are not required to publish your contact information, as long as you provide a way for potential employers to contact you, preferably with a contact form on your website. A contact form allows the interested party to contact you, by providing *their* name, email address, and a confidential message, without disclosing your personal contact information. Like the rest of your website, your online resume page should be updated often too.

You can also post your resume on career websites such as Monster and CareerBuilder if you are interested in a more permanent writing position. This allows your resume to be searched at any time, if you so choose. You have many options available to you on these websites: You can set the visibility level of your resume to public or private and you can change the visibility level at any time. You can apply to positions on the career websites using your already uploaded resume, which is fast and easy. You can provide additional information about yourself, such as your goals, and awards and acknowledgements you have received.

A Beginning Writer's Resume

Since you are reading this book, you are probably new to professional writing or you wish to begin, so you'll likely need to create a beginning writer's resume. A beginning writer's resume will help you to obtain clients or to apply for freelance writing jobs. The main actions you'll want to take with your resume are to highlight your skills and include writing samples.

Objective Statement

The first part of the resume is the "objective," which is a one or two-phrase statement that states what type of job you are seeking and what you can contribute to an organization. Be concise, use vivid adjectives and action verbs, and make it sound attractive, so that the manager will want to read further. It is to be short and sweet.

An example of an objective statement is: To achieve a freelance position as a resume writer at a growing company where I can contribute my ambition and my flawless writing skills.

Highlight Your Skills

Next, you should "brainstorm" ideas to come up with as many skills as possible that you have related to freelance writing. These skills could be along the lines of researching, outlining, drafting, composing, revising, editing, and proofreading—which are essentially the steps to completing a piece of writing.

You might want to include typing skills and typing speed, computer programs you're familiar with, websites or blogs you run, and independent or consulting work you've done. Write down everything that comes to mind. By doing this, you will reveal some skills you didn't realize you had.

Then you can edit and refine your skills. When you add your skills to your resume, start each line off with an action verb, include only one skill per line, and use short phrases.

Education Section

A college degree is an excellent item to put in the education section, but it is not the only piece you can include. Be open-minded with this section. Any college class you've taken can be included in the education section, especially if it is relevant to writing. This can also include free courses or classes at a past employer. Certificates can also be included in this section. But make sure it was from a class, otherwise it would be considered an award, which is part of the next section.

Awards and Accomplishments

Awards and accomplishments are usually education or employment-based. Academic or professional achievements should be included in this section. It could be anything from honors or Dean's List to saving a past company money or a substantial promotion. Any time you received recognition for your behavior, especially if it was related to writing, it can be incorporated in this section.

Work Experience or Work History

If you already have work experience that is related to writing, definitely include that information on your resume. If you don't have any writing experience, you can still list your employers, job titles, and dates of employment, but put it last on your resume, since it is best to put the most relevant and strongest points first. Or, you can integrate your work history with your skills or accomplishments to flesh it out and connect it to the writing theme.

***

That's all there is to it. Now you can post your resume on job boards or your website, and it's ready for submitting to writing positions.

Your resume represents you as a person and a professional, as well as all you have to offer the prospective company, so put forth effort to make it high-quality and polished. Treat it like other pieces of writing you do by editing and proofreading it for errors.

Chapter 13
Cover Letters

Cover letters are pretty much the same format for everyone, however, there is room for creativity. It is a good skill to know how to write a cover letter, which is what this chapter will show you. You might just need a refresher on your cover letter writing skills. Or you may need to create a cover letter from scratch. Either way, hopefully the examples provided in this chapter that are tailored to writing careers will be helpful.

Purposes of a Cover Letter

The first purpose of a cover letter is to introduce the potential employer to your resume and/or employment application. Ideally, the cover letter accompanies your resume, and possibly an employment application, whether in print or online.

The second purpose of a cover letter is to introduce yourself to the employer as a potential employee. The cover letter is the first aspect of yourself, as a job candidate for a writing position, that a possible client or manager will see. It is usually their first impression of you, since you will probably not come face-to-face with the person who will decide to call you for an interview when you drop off your cover letter and resume or application. These hiring managers usually work behind the scenes. And if you applied online, you will likely not speak to the hiring manager until you are called for an interview.

A cover letter is your sales pitch. It introduces yourself, gets and holds the reader's attention, provides information about your work history and experience, and closes with a hint for an interview. Let's review the parts to a cover letter in more detail so that you will be able to compose your own cover letter.

The Introduction

Every piece of writing must have a beginning, and a cover letter is no different. The introduction of a cover letter can be from a sentence up to a paragraph; it depends on your approach. For instance, if you know someone at the company and you have a referral (a current employee, at the company you are applying to, that recommends to the hiring manage that he/she consider you for a job opening), the introduction may be a bit longer than one sentence, because you have additional information to provide.

Generally, the introduction will say how you heard about the position, and that you are interested in the position and working for the company. You can also reflect briefly on what you know about the company in a casual way to show you've done your research. You can also include the name of your referral and their job title.

It is important to keep the introduction short, because you don't want to lose your reader's interest. So be clear, concise, and direct, and move on to the meat of the cover letter.

Reader's Attention

Holding the reader's attention is important so that the hiring manager will be interested in you as a job candidate. If the manager gets bored halfway through reading your cover letter, they may dismiss your application altogether. To hold the reader's attention, use transitional words and phrases to keep the message flowing quickly and easily. Continue to be clear and concise, so the manager will understand you well. And use strong verbs and descriptions that are related to the job position so that the reader will find you as a fit for the job, and that acknowledgement will make him or her interested in you, which is a very good thing when applying for jobs.

Work History

Be general and brief when providing your work history. Highlight the key points. Your work history is already listed on your resume, so you don't need to recite it exactly. You can generalize and also mention events that you did *not* list on your resume that are intriguing, such as lessons you learned and unique aspects of the positions you held. You should tie it in with the job you are applying for, by making your experiences relate to the job duties of the prospective position as much as possible.

A good technique is to re-word the work history section of your resume, to have it look unique on your cover letter, by stating total years worked in each career field. It is a good way to state your experience concisely that will look good to the hiring manager.

Accomplishments

Mentioning your accomplishments is a helpful way to build interest and maintain the manager's attention. Don't be afraid to "show off." This is the time to brag about your accomplishments. The manager won't know that you are really fast at typing or editing, or how many articles you can write in an hour, unless you tell them those facts. They will definitely be impressed if you do.

Closing

Wrap up the cover letter with a "thank you for your time" or "thank you for considering my resume/application." Tell them when you are available for an interview, or when you can best be reached to discuss the position further. Close the cover letter by saying you look forward to speaking with them soon.

The Angle

A cover letter is similar to a sales letter in that you want to persuade the reader into hiring you for a writing position. In order to do so, you will need to be direct and assertive in your language. Do not be afraid to tell them you are interested in the job; do not be afraid to highlight your achievements; and do not be afraid to say you look forward to an interview. This is *not* the time to be shy or passive.

Don’t forget to put your best foot forward. Therefore, do not talk about negative situations in the past. Instead, be positive and optimistic about the job you are applying for and your accomplishments. Be professional and friendly in your written voice. Keep the manager’s interest so that they will want to evaluate your resume to learn more about you.

PART 4

EDUCATE YOURSELF

Chapter 14
Writing Courses

Do you think that high school is enough education for being a writer? Think again. There is so much to learn and so much experience to gain in the world of writing and the English language. College is the perfect place to acquire discipline to write long papers, and learn the technicalities of proofreading.

Now that you've decided to be a writer, school will benefit you so much more than before you wanted to write, because you'll be trying harder and paying more attention to your studies. Plus, adult college students tend to do better than young students, because they have life skills and maturity that makes them want to focus more on getting good grades. Having a different focus affects everything.

There are different ways to approach getting additional education for your writing skills. There are free courses, online courses, campus-based courses, certificate programs, online degrees, and campus-based degrees. Let's look at those options closer to see which one will be right for you.

Free Courses

Free courses are out there if you look for them. Here are some websites that provide links to free college courses:

- *Open Culture*: They have a list of over 400 free online courses in liberal arts and sciences that are audio and video downloads. You can take the class at home—on your computer or laptop—or on-the-go on your mp3 player.
- *Education Insider*: If you scroll down the webpage a little, there is a list of the "top free online schools," each with their own link. These courses include assignments and lecture notes.

Keep in mind that with these free courses, you won't be in touch with other students or professors; you would need to purchase the books to get the full benefit; and you won't get college credits for taking the courses. It would be a very independent venture, but if you like to write, read, and study independently, it is something worth considering. If it's free and you gain something from it, you have come out on top!

Online Courses

Online courses that you pay for are highly interactive with chat, messaging, professors, other students, live video, assignments, quizzes, and discussions. You will need to buy the book(s) required for each class. You will get college credit for them. You should make sure the college is accredited, at least regionally, or else the credits won't count if you decide to transfer to a different college. You can apply for financial aid, or pay out-of-pocket, but make sure you don't get over your head in debt, because these classes can be pricey.

Online courses are perfect for students who learn best by reading and writing. There is a lot of textbook reading and reading on the computer, as well as discussion posts, writing assignments, and virtual quizzes. You must be independent and driven to take an online course. You will never meet your instructors or students, but this is acceptable nowadays with people being so used to the Internet and doing everything online.

Campus-Based Courses

With campus-based courses, you will need to arrive at class on time and in person. You will likely sit amongst a number of different students, and that number can vary greatly. Then your instructor will arrive and begin the lecture. He or she will ask the class (all the students as a whole) questions about what they've been studying. Most of the time will be spent with the instructor covering new information and then sending you home with reading to do and assignments to complete. The instructor will collect your assignments the day they are due.

You must stay on top of your studying and written assignments. You can schedule to meet with your instructor if you are struggling, or have a question that you didn't get to ask, or didn't get answered, during class.

The classes are held at different times of the day. You will need to purchase writing supplies, folders, and textbooks. You have less time for studying than with online courses, because you must attend classes in person, which takes up significant time sitting in class as well as time spent on commuting, weather conditions, parking, traffic, etc.

If you like to be around a lot of people and have face-to-face interactions and discussions, plus the accountability of having to be at class regularly, then campus-based courses are for you.

Certificate Programs

Certificates can be achieved both online and on campus. Certificates are like degrees, except less courses are required to obtain them and they are not as prestigious as degrees. However, they hold more prestige than free courses or taking a single course—online or on campus. Some certificates can be achieved by taking one or two courses.

If you'd like to earn a tangible reward for your hard work as a student, but don't want to complete a degree because of the length of time it takes to achieve, a certificate is a good method of obtaining an education and completing a program.

Certificates can help you in the workplace and in your career as a freelance writer. The knowledge you gain from earning the certificate is sometimes more important than the certificate itself, because as a freelance writer, your first concern is writing and communicating well. Therefore, take courses that will improve your craft and business knowledge, rather than try to earn a certificate just to have one. The knowledge is much more beneficial and profitable.

Online Degrees

Online degrees are similar to online classes, except that the classes you take must fulfill a degree program and be accredited. You will be required to take a specific number of classes and certain types. Online colleges have different program requisites and different degrees. Find the degree that most fits you and the type of courses that you like the best. Some courses are four, six, or eight weeks long, and some online colleges are affiliated with a campus-based college. If you look at the course catalog, you can decide which classes and degree program you like best.

Then you must go through the enrollment period, which requires confirming payment arrangements and getting your transcripts (which is usually simple, because the school requests them for you). Then you get assigned a class and can order your textbook(s). Textbooks for online classes can be cheap, depending on if you get used ones and where you buy them.

Then you log into your course, which you should do every day to keep abreast of new posts, assignments, and instructions. There will likely be new posts daily and you won't want to fall behind on the course content. The best part is you can quickly check in on your course from any computer and at any time. You can get the information you need and spend as little or as much time as needed on your course, depending on what type of grade you want and the demands of the course.

Online courses are typically fast-paced. Normally, you only need to take one course at a time to be considered a full-time student and the courses only last for several weeks. You will need to reach out to your professor and classmates by asking questions if and when you struggle, and also for participation credit (some instructors count participation as a small percentage of the overall grade). When you complete a quiz, you will likely not be able to take it again to improve your grade, so be conscientious when answering the questions.

The toughest part of all is finding the motivation and desire to complete all of your classes. It can take years to earn an online degree, so take that into consideration before attempting it. Once you earn your degree, however, you will be a happy camper.

Campus-Based Degrees

Campus-based degrees are a lot of work. You will usually take several courses at a time and go to them for months, which is equaled to a semester. Then you will get a schedule for your next semester. You will attend each course as explained above under "campus-based courses," until you complete the required number of courses and credits for your degree. This takes years to do. So, make sure you are certain you want to spend that much time earning your education, and make sure you pick the right degree program that will interest you and benefit you most.

The Important Part

The most important part about education is not the diploma that says you graduated, but the knowledge you take with you from the learning experience. You are a career-minded individual now and your first concern is performing your job duties as a freelance writer. The education you decide to pursue should be used for your business and to improve your craft. Not many classes are needed to do that. You may look at taking a creative writing course if you think it will be beneficial. It may be all you need to further succeed as a freelance writer.

Types of Courses

Writing involves a lot of different skills, so there are many different types of courses you could take.

There are: English language courses, such as English Mechanics (grammar, spelling, punctuation), English Composition (writing papers, including a works cited, and conducting research), and English Vocabulary (definitions, synonyms, antonyms). There are courses that teach you about the specifics of editing and proofreading. There are also courses that instruct on techniques involved with technical writing, copy writing, script writing, poetry writing, prose writing, etc. Or you may venture to take communications, journalism, or business courses.

Is education a requirement for being a freelance writer? No. But it also can't hurt. Taking certain courses might help you touch up your spelling or grammar issues or improve your style so that you can make more money. The better writer you are, the more money you will make.

Chapter 15

Reading and Writing Book Reviews

Reading can be a leisurely activity, a method of research, a way to get educated, or a way to improve your writing skills. Reading takes a person to a different time, place, or world; provides valuable knowledge; improves memory and concentration; keeps a person's mind sharp; and provides a person the means to teach him or herself, or to be taught.

When you read, and comprehend the majority of the words and their meaning, you learn. When you read, you absorb information, and it is impossible for it to not have an impact on your thoughts. In fact, you are a different person from each book you read. You learn new methods, new insights, new perspectives, new information. The act of reading is a powerful tool that you should feel privileged to be able to do, because it can do so much for you in your lifetime.

Reading as a Writer

When you read as a writer, you will improve your grammar, spelling, and vocabulary. Since you are a writer, it will be hard for you to *not* pay attention, because when you read, you review what you already do for a living, what you love to do, and who you are! You will no longer race through books riding the storyline. You will read astutely, noticing the author's techniques, and you will probably even pick up on the mistakes they make.

Now that you are a writer, reading will never be the same to you. But, it is a good thing. You will learn and enjoy, while reading a book, rather than just enjoy. You will improve your craft, rather than just breeze through the pages to never see them again. Reading will have more of a purpose and will be more meaningful. You will be able to enjoy the story, but you will take more importance away from it than if you weren't a writer.

Purposes of Reading

As a writer, reading can be for enjoyment, to improve your skills, to learn, and to research. Reading is the perfect activity for busy writers to do to relax, because they are also being productive! Curl up with a book of your choosing, and when you're done, possibly write a book review (talked about below).

Read to observe the skills of other writers and it will inspire you to improve your own style. Read to learn, to educate yourself or others, or to be educated by someone, such as in a classroom or at home.

Lastly, read to do research for writing an essay, an article, a school paper, a short story, or a book. Researching is a method of education that will advance your knowledge and perspective on life. You will never be the same once you receive information and digest it, for it will affect your outlook in the present, your experiences in the future, and possibly your memories of the past.

So try reading to take a break from writing, to learn and enhance your writing skills, and to perform research to be used in your reports, stories, and novels.

You will probably like the experience of reading, even if you didn't like it in the past. You may need to try out different genres and topics, but eventually you will find one that fits your tastes. And because you are forever growing and changing, your reading tastes will change too. Give reading a chance!

Book Reviews

Now that you've done all that reading, you might as well use it to your advantage: write a book review. The author will thank you, and you will have a new clip for your portfolio. In the beginning, you can publish it on your blog, in a reading community, or at the website of the store you purchased it from.

Writing a book review is not too challenging; after all, it is basically your interpretation of the book and your opinion about it. Although, the writing should be organized and tactful, and free of errors.

There are as many different ways to write a book review as there are book reviewers and books. You should put your own personal style into it, and find a method that works well for you.

You will also probably find that each of your book reviews is arranged slightly different. That's okay. That means you are going with the flow of how the book affected you and the type of book it is, which are different for each book.

Structure of a Book Review

Even though the structure of a book review is relaxed and flexible, it should still be somewhat organized. There should be one idea per paragraph, and the paragraphs should be in a logical sequence. Use transitions to guide the reader from paragraph to paragraph, so that the flow isn't choppy. Here is one structure of a book review:

- *First paragraph*: Introduce book and author with complete title and name. Provide an interesting first or second sentence that will make the reader interested in your review. Compose a general statement—of one sentence—telling what the book is like.
- *Second paragraph*: Introduce the book with a short sentence that leads into the book's storyline. Write several sentences about the

contents of the book or the storyline, mostly from the beginning, so as not to ruin the ending for the reader. Do not give away the story climax or ending. Just provide the basics of the plot and talk a bit about the main characters.

- *Third paragraph*: Give your opinion of the book in several sentences, providing examples that support your claims. Be fair and tactful with sharing your opinion, and hold a level of objectiveness. Do not hold judgments against the author or style of the book, or other things that might sway your judgment of the content of the book, which is what the book review should be based on. If there are a lot of spelling or grammatical errors in the book, it is best to save that for the star score, not to point out in the review.
- *Fourth paragraph*: State directly if you would recommend the book to others or not. Provide a yes or no answer based on your general feel of the book. If you are unsure, you can write that you recommend the book to readers of ______ (genre). Then provide a concluding sentence or

two to wrap up the review. You might mention where you can buy the book (if the review is posted on your blog or website) and provide direct links. It's better to end the review quickly, rather than to drag on, because reviews are supposed to be short and to-the-point.

***

Now you're ready to write a book review, so go find a good book, spend some time reading the *whole* thing (that's important for a fair and complete review), and write a review afterwards. You'll want to write the review soon after you finish the book, so that your impression and the storyline are fresh in your mind.

Chapter 16

Search Engine Optimization

Search engine optimization (SEO) is a phrase used on the Web that writers who have blogs and websites should know well. When you publish articles and blog posts, you will want them to appear near the top of the search engine results so that you get the most traffic (visitors). That is the main importance of SEO.

SEO changes as search engines change how they sort their search results. There is an abundant amount of information online about SEO—you just have to look (at the end of this chapter there are links to helpful websites on SEO).

Currently, the best SEO practices include: using keywords, limiting outbound links, putting the most important information at the top of each webpage, making sure all internal links work correctly, and not having too many flashy advertisements. Let's review those one at a time. (For the sake of brevity, "website" refers to blogs as well.)

Using Keywords

Keywords are a large part of SEO. Keywords are every word on a website that means something to the search engines. The most important places to focus on keywords are in the URL, title of the website, individual webpage titles, subtitles, and content. When putting words into these areas of your website, choose accurate words that reflect your meaning and purpose. These words will be found by the search engines in order to provide accurate results for those searching the Web. So, choose strong adjectives, nouns, and verbs. You can also add tags (keywords that highlight what a blog post is about), and the same rules as keywords applies.

Limit Outbound Links

It's helpful to have outbound links on your website, because it tells the search engines that you are involved in the community of the Web. However, don't get carried away with adding links, because too many links makes a website look like spam to the search engines, so they won't rank your website as high in the search results. The outbound links you choose to use should be reputable websites, because it makes *your* website look reputable.

Put Important Keywords at the Top

When someone uses a search engine to research a topic, the search engine takes the words the person submits, scans all websites for those words, and puts forth a list of links to the web pages that have those words on their pages in order of relevancy (words closest to the keyword) and quantity (number of times keyword is repeated on the webpage).

When the search engine scans websites, it starts at the top of each webpage and doesn't scan everything on the page. Therefore, it is recommended to put your important keywords first and at the top of the page.

This means you will also want to avoid putting graphics above your content, because the search engines only look for words, so the graphics will slow down its scanning process and it might decide to skip to the next page.

Internal Links Work Correctly

There are at least several internal links for each website, which are words that you click on your website that lead to another page on your website. These words can be found in the directory tabs at the top, links in the sidebars, links at the bottom of web pages, and links within the content.

Make sure all of the links work correctly so that search engines can properly scan your website for keywords. Search engines follow all links to where they lead, so if the search engine comes to a dead link, it could stop scanning your website and go on to the next website.

It is easy to make sure all of the links work correctly. Occasionally, click on the internal links and confirm they lead where they are supposed to, rather than to a dead page or the wrong page.

In addition, you should check your outbound links to make sure they lead to the correct places as well. A bunch of dead or faulty links—both internal and outbound—signals to search engines that the website is not maintained properly, possibly because it is old and the information is outdated, so they will not place those websites near the top of the search results.

Avoid Flashy Ads

Ads are outbound links, and as stated previously, you don't want to have an over-abundance of them, because it looks like spam to the search engines. Flashy ads are even more problematic, because they send the message to search engines that the website is not reputable and it won't end up ranking high in the search results.

Helpful Web Pages

For more information about SEO, feel free to visit the following websites:

- *Google Support Webmasters*: Search Engine Optimization (SEO)

- *Search Engine Land*: What is SEO / Search Engine Optimization?

For a free SEO online course, webinar, and tutorial, visit the following websites:

- *HubPages*: Free Online SEO Training Course
- *Jason McDonald*: Free SEO Tools Webinar
- *HTP Company*: Free SEO Tutorial

PART 5

HELPFUL TOOLS FOR YOUR BUSINESS

Chapter 17
Equipment and Supplies

It's important to have the right tools for the job. There are a lot of different tools you will need as a freelance writer. But you can start by acquiring the basics and then slowly add to your supplies.

Writers have different needs as far as what tools they prefer. When you first start out, all you need is paper, a writing utensil, and a comfortable chair. Next, you may decide to get a small table light and notebooks. Then you may upgrade to a word-processing device, computer, or laptop, an Internet connection, and a desk. Next, you might invest in a printer (with copier, scanner, and fax preferably). Finally, you will want to get a filing cabinet and filing supplies. Hopefully, within a year, you will have all of the above.

Let's go over each of the tools to show what they can do and their importance:

Paper and a Writing Utensil

You are a writer if you believe you are, and have paper and a writing utensil. Freelance writers use paper and pens all the time, especially for jotting down ideas for novels, articles, and blog posts, or taking notes about a business phone call. As a new freelance writer, you will probably start with these supplies. They get the job done when you want to write. Some writers who have moved on to using a computer, still write their first drafts out by hand using traditional pen and paper.

Comfortable Chair

This is crucial. You'll likely be sitting for a long time (hours) when you write, so a comfortable chair will help tremendously. You will notice how writing becomes uncomfortable if you don't have a good chair that will support you for long periods.

You will have to find what type of chair you like best. A kitchen chair, a lounge chair, a computer chair, a sofa, a bed, etc. Figure out if you want a chair with arm rests or perhaps one that reclines. Having a comfortable chair will allow you to stay focused on your writing.

Table Light

Because of most people's commitments during the day—day job, homecare, children, errands—many writers will find their writing time will be at night. Maybe your family is sleeping and you don't want to disturb them, but you want to continue writing. That is when a small table light comes in handy. You'll be able to write for as long as you want and won't have to stop when you are in the midst of a good part of the story or before you finish your article or blog post.

Notebook

Instead of loose paper, you might decide to get a notebook or two. A notebook will keep your writing organized. It is easiest to write in a notebook that lies flat, so look for the spiral-bound kind. You might find that keeping small notebooks in various places will allow you to write down ideas that come to you during the day; that way you won't forget your idea by the time you get around to writing it down, because a notebook will already be handy. You can keep a notebook beside your bed, in your car, in your pocket or purse, and even in each room of your house for convenience.

Word-Processing Device, Laptop, or Desktop Computer

Now that you've got all sorts of ideas and articles written down, you will want to type them up. If you can, you should invest in a word-processing device at the very least. If possible, save up for a laptop or desktop computer (preferably a laptop, because you can bring it with you wherever you go). With a laptop or computer you will need word-processing software. You can get it for free from the Open Office website.

Internet Connection

Then it is time to publish your writing, so you will need an Internet connection. Your choices are dial-up

($7-10/month) and broadband ($20+/month). A dial-up connection uses your telephone line to connect to the Internet. There are different types of broadband Internet: DSL, Cable, Fiber-Optic, Satellite, and Wireless. Research your options to find the one that is most beneficial to you.

You need an Internet connection to publish your writing, whether you want to publish articles to content websites, posts to your blog, or ebooks. With an Internet connection, you can join online writing communities and social networking websites, and have your own blog and website.

Desk

Now is a good time to upgrade the kitchen table, or wherever you've been writing, to a desk. It will give you more room to store your laptop and will allow you to keep your supplies all in one place. Plus, a desk is more professional and will make you *feel* more professional, which might help you with your career. Move some furniture around to make room for your new desk.

Printer

A printer is very helpful if you need to print pages from your computer. As a freelance writer, you will need to keep track of your income and expenses (covered in the next chapter) for tax purposes, and having a paper copy is a good idea for filing with your tax documents. Some printers also come with the capability for copying, scanning, and faxing. You don't need to invest in one of those, but you will probably want to eventually, so if you can afford it now, it's a good idea to get one.

Filing Cabinet and Supplies

You will need to file papers, if you don't already, so get yourself a file cabinet. It can be a small, portable, cardboard one that is shaped like an accordion when you open it, a large plastic one, or a metal one that stays at home and has drawers. Get a file cabinet based on your filing needs, how much you need to file, and what you have room for in your home, since file cabinets can take up a lot of space. Keep everything organized in the file cabinet and go through the paperwork twice a year to toss out any paperwork you don't need any more.

***

Now that you have all the supplies you need, you're all set to continue your writing career!

Chapter 18

Tracking Income and Expenses

If you enjoy personal finance, keeping track of your income and expenses will be fun. Otherwise, it will be a chore and may seem to damper your creative spirit. But, you can think of it as being organized and accountable for your career. It is a part of being a freelance writer.

Why Keep Track of Work Performed

In the first year of freelance writing, you should keep track of your work duties if you plan to claim yourself as self-employed on your taxes. The reason being is if you have more expenses than income—which sometimes happens with start-up businesses—you'll have a record of all the work you've done, in case you are ever audited and need to show proof of your business, rather than someone who claims expenses but doesn't put effort into their business. You may not get audited, but it's a good idea to be prepared in case you do.

Income as a Freelance Writer

You may be financially successful right off the bat. But it's not common, because, like chapters prior to this one reflect, it takes time to enhance your writing skills, gain knowledge about the business of freelance writing, build a portfolio, and accumulate enough published pieces to make substantial money.

In a couple of years your business will be more worthwhile to you. And if it doesn't become fruitful, you will at least have a career doing what you love, and *that* makes it worthwhile. However, if you are interested in a lot of income right from the start, and that's all that matters to you, then freelance writing is probably not for you. For those of you that have to support yourself right away, you can focus on selecting the highest paying opportunities of those found in previous chapters of this book.

That being said, you still need to keep track of your finances for tax purposes and for peace of mind. The following sections will show you how.

Create a Simple Budget Chart

Keeping track of your finances is something you should already be doing as a member of a household. You need to know how to budget your money and save money. To easily do this, make a list of all your bills and expenses, and try not to forget any. Round up to the nearest dollar or five dollar increment. If you have an expense that is not paid monthly, simply divide the total bill by the number of months the expense covers. For example, a quarterly bill covers three months of expenses, so a $120 bill would need to be divide by 3. Therefore, you can put $40 as the monthly expense for that bill.

Next, make a list of your income sources. Don't leave anything out. You want to take full advantage of all the income you have so that you can save as much as possible, if that is your objective. At the very least, you will want an accurate representation of your income. Now, total the income and expenses separately.

Subtract the expenses from the income total. The total you get is the extra money you have that you can choose to save or spend, or both.

Income and Expenses Chart

Now that you have a budget chart, you can make a chart of your income and expenses for your writing business. It is best to have all charts on a computer spreadsheet eventually. Make the far-left column for listing the type of income or business expense it is. The next column (to the right) will be for listing the amounts for individual income sources as they come in. The next column will be for listing the amounts of individual business expenses. In the next column, you will write a general label for the business expenses; for example: supplies, internet connection, marketing, research, other, etc. At the bottom, you can total the columns for income and expense amounts to determine monthly income and monthly expenses.

Work Activities Chart

Next, you should make a chart of your monthly work activities, because, like mentioned previously, it is a good idea to have a record of what work you do for your business for tax purposes. Create a new chart for every calendar month. Make the far-left column for the date, the next column for the type of work activity you did, and the third column for notes you need to add. Every time you perform work related activities, such as publishing your writing or working on your manuscripts, write them down.

Writing Time Chart

The next chart you can make is for tracking the amount of time you spend writing and the number of words that you do. Make the first column for the date, the second column for the time period you wrote, the third column for what you accomplished (for example, wrote/edit chapters 1-3 or pages 50-70), and the fourth column for the number of words you completed. Fill in an entry for each writing session.

***

Those are the basic charts that you will need to maintain. Feel free to alter them or add to them to make them most helpful for your needs. Remember to keep track of your business as much as possible. It's better to have more records than you need than not enough.

Computer Files and Folders

Keep your charts and writing organized in your computer by naming the files in a concise way that you'll be able to tell exactly what it is before you open the file. Make folders to organize the files. Put the files into the right folders. It's pretty simple. But you'll also want to keep up with the system so that you'll be able to find everything you're looking for all the time. If the name of the file or folder needs to be changed to be more accurate, you can do so by right-clicking the name, selecting "rename," typing in the name you want, and hitting the enter key.

Receipts and Documents

When you need to purchase items for your business, make sure you do separate transactions for your business items. Save all of your business receipts. Make a copy of the receipt and attach the original to the copy—in order to save the original but to also have a copy, because the ink on receipts can fade with time.

Print out copies of your work and your charts every month. Put all paperwork in a monthly folder. Save the folders in a file cabinet until tax time comes around. Then you will be all organized and prepared to file your taxes!

PART 6

A WRITER'S LIFESTYLE

Chapter 19
A Lifestyle Change

No matter what you do for work, becoming a freelance writer is going to be a huge change. No other job is like it. You will work long hours, sit at the computer for hours at a time, get less sleep, drink more coffee, and spend a lot of time alone as you write.

Working a Lot

If you wish to succeed as a freelance writer, in the first year you will work all day and all week. You will feel like you are tied to the computer. There will be so much work to do and not enough time to do it. You will be multitasking projects like crazy. It will be very hard to tie up all the loose ends in one day. You will have projects that take more than one day, such as book review assignments, which take several days or weeks. Hopefully you don't mind working hard, long hours or not having all your projects complete at the end of every day. It's just not going to happen. The reality is you will probably work up to 12 hours a day and up to 7 days a week and will still have work left over for the next day. But if you love writing, you really won't mind.

Working Alone

Writing work is usually done alone. When you write you can't do anything but write. You can't talk to someone, or pick things up, or watch TV. Writing requires your full concentration and all your fingertips. There's no way around it. Because you won't able to interact with others when you're writing, you'll likely work alone.

You'll also be working from home which brings its own distractions and complications (will be discussed in the next chapter). If you are independent and enjoy time alone, you will be just fine.

Less Sleep

Sleep is very important. But if you're in the middle of editing an article and you have a deadline, sleep can wait.

Being a freelance writer involves a unique "busyness." Freelance writers tend to be quick and active thinkers and productive people. Writing a lot can make some people hyperactive and unable to sleep.

Even the non-writing parts of a freelance writing career—such as marketing, promotion, social networking, and reading—can be done in this hyperactive state.

Inspiration comes and goes on a daily basis, so when you have a great idea or feel inclined to write, you'll write really fast and get deeply involved in your writing for as long as the inspiration is there.

Often you will get involved in a project and not want to stop when it's your usual bedtime. Then, if you have a family and have to get up early the next morning to tend to things, the writing you did the night before ends up cutting into some of your morning sleep time.

However, if you really need the rest, take it. You should try to get approximately eight hours of sleep each night. This is just a warning that your sleep schedule may change a bit and it may be your choice.

Coffee Consumption

If you have commitments besides writing, you might find yourself writing in the early morning, late at night, or both. If you are a coffee drinker and need coffee to get up in the mornings, and you get up extra early to write, you will probably want extra coffee to keep your mind alert. If you are writing late at night, you might find that you drink more coffee during the day or night in order to stay up late at night.

This is just a fair warning that your coffee consumption will probably increase. Of course, it doesn't have to—it's up to you.

Computer Time

You will definitely be spending a lot of time on the computer to do your work, because your job duties will be almost 100% done on the computer. So if your family shares a computer, you should consider getting an extra computer or laptop so that you will have plenty of time and opportunity to do your work, and your family members will be able to continue using a computer.

You will probably get tired of sitting at the computer if you've been there for hours. You can take a break to read, watch television, or better yet—exercise. Write and work for as long as you can at the computer, and then when you need a break, you won't feel guilty about taking one.

Casual Living

When you work from home you do not have to dress professionally, or shower for that matter. You will probably "go to work" in casual clothes or your pajamas even. You don't need to go out of the house, unless you have appointments, so there's no need for wearing makeup or jewelry either. If this all sounds good to you, you will enjoy being a freelance writer.

Positives of Being a Freelance Writer

There are many positives of being a freelance writer:

- You can work from home
- You can have a flexible work schedule
- You can do work you enjoy that doesn't seem like work
- You can be home with your spouse, children, or pets
- You can work in comfortable surroundings
- You don't have to commute to work
- You don't have to get ready for work
- You are your own boss.

Chapter 20

Be Assertive About Your Career Needs

Working from home is great, but it also comes with challenges. There are a lot of distractions at home, like previously mentioned, such as: phone, television, spouse, kids, pets, visitors. The lack of structure from not having to be at a job location might make you feel like doing other things, like going out to the mall or going to the beach. So you must be disciplined and state your needs for alone time to others in your household, so that you can get your work done.

Alone Time

It's a good idea to sit down with your family and explain to them what your new career entails. Explain to them that you will be spending a lot of time writing, researching, reading, and networking, and it all takes your full concentration. Tell them what your needs are, such as: “if the office door is closed, don’t disturb”; “write down messages for me when people call for me, and save them for the end of the day, rather than telling me each time I have a phone call”; “the hours I need privately are 8-11 am and 8-11 pm Monday through Friday”; etc. You can also tell your family to pretend you are not home, so that they can be the ones to regularly answer the door and phone instead.

Ask for Help

Not only do you need alone time, you will also need help with your children, your pets, and the household. You won’t have as much time to watch the children, take care of the pets, clean the house, do the shopping, and run errands. You will need help from other people in your family. If everyone can take on an extra responsibility, it wouldn’t be much of a burden for them, but it would lighten your load tremendously. Don’t be afraid to state your needs and ask for help.

Create Charts

You can create charts for your family to help them remember what you discussed when you confronted them about your need for help and alone time. Create a calendar for your work schedule that shows when you will be on the computer, taking phone calls, reading, filing, etc., and include your days and hours off. Secondly, design a chart that lists household chores, when to do them, and who's responsible for each. Hang up both charts where everyone will see them (the refrigerator is a good place). You'll be amazed how much a visual representation will help them and you.

Chapter 21

Income and Payment

In your first year as a freelance writer, income is little to none. But if you are looking to be in this career long-term, there is the possibility to earn greater income.

Since you are reading this book, it is safe to assume that you love to write and read. The joy of fulfilling your dreams is a great benefit of being a freelance writer. Doing what you love every day is worth more than doing something you dislike. Some writers take a cut in pay in order to be happy. You will have to decide what is most important to you: money or happiness.

There are, however, many opportunities to make money in your first year as a freelance writer. There is pay from articles, ads on your web pages, ghostwriting, and selling books.

Article Pay

Writers who write articles for content websites typically get three types of pay, but not necessarily all three at once. These are: revenue share, page views, and upfront payments.

Revenue Share

Generally speaking, when a website owner decides to put advertisements on their website, and a visitor clicks on one of their ads and buys something, the website owner earns a percentage of the profits from the visitor's purchase.

Content websites that host your published articles put ads on the web pages that your articles are on that are related to your articles' topics. Since people read articles on the Web about topics that interest them, they will be more inclined to click on the ads on the page, because they are similar to the topic that initially interested them.

When the person clicks on an ad and buys something, the content website earns money and you will get a percentage of their share. This amount will accrue in your account until you decide to receive payment from it. You can only receive payment after you reach a monetary threshold that is determined by the content website.

Page Views

Some content websites pay their writers based on page views. Each time a person views one of your articles, you will accrue page views which turns into pay. The average pay for page views is $1.50 for every 1,000 views.

In contrast to revenue share, visitors don't even have to click on the ads and buy something; just viewing your article will earn you some income.

Page view pay accrues until you decide to cash it out. First you must reach the monetary threshold that is determined by the content website and is different for each website.

Upfront Payments

Many articles are urgent (i.e. for news, a new season, a new holiday coming up, etc.), requested by the content website, or a "hot" (very popular) topic. Writers of these types of articles are sometimes paid separate one-time payments called "upfront payments." Upfront payments can range from $1 to $15 or more. The payment is in addition to revenue share or page view pay. So upfront payments are like a bonus. If you have the option to obtain an upfront payment, definitely do so.

Website Advertisements

You have the option to put ads on your blog or website. If you do so, you will accrue funds in an account with the ad company you use when visitors click on your ads and make a purchase.

Common websites that provide ads include:

- *Google AdSense*: This is a free program in which you can earn revenue by displaying relevant ads on your website.
- *Google Affiliate*: This is a free program that will allow you to connect with quality advertisers

and get paid when visitors click on the ads on your website and make a purchase.

- *Amazon Associates*: You can earn a percentage of advertising fees when visitors to your website click on ads that are from your Amazon Associates account. The profit percentage range is about 4-15%.
- *Click Bank*: When you put up company ads—that you choose—on your website, you can earn up to 75% commission.

(The above information was derived from the companies' websites.)

Ghostwriting

Ghostwriting often pays more than articles that you write for content websites. This is because, when you ghostwrite you do not get your name published with your article, so it equals out that you get an extra financial "incentive" for losing the rights to your work. The main ghostwriting website—where you are almost always guaranteed immediate work and that nearly anyone can join—is Textbroker.

Textbroker pays 0.7 cents per word and up, depending on what writing level you are. The writing level is determined by the quality of your writing sample from your online application. As a Textbroker writer, the more quality articles that you write, the greater the chance you have of increasing your writing level and earning higher pay per word.

There are opportunities to earn even more money with team projects. For example, some team projects pay up to 31 cents per word.

On a side note, if you state on your professional website that you do ghostwriting services, people searching the Web for a ghostwriter may contact you for your services and the pay would likely be moderate to high.

Selling Books

If you like to write books as a freelance writer, you can make money after they are published. You can join websites like Lulu or CreateSpace (by Amazon) to produce and sell print copies of your books. You can join Smashwords and Kindle Direct Publishing to create and sell ebook versions of your books. You can also, of course, query an agent or publisher to get traditionally published. If your books are well-written, well-presented, and get good reviews, you could profit very well from being an author.

***

You might only make pennies per day at first, but your income will grow. If you put a lot of time and effort into your writing business, someday you will be able to support yourself on your writing income alone.

Afterword

If you were destined to be a writer, you naturally feel drawn to the act of writing. You are not able to avoid doing it. You enjoy articulating words onto the page. You love to share your thoughts, feelings, ideas, aspirations, characters, stories, and poems with anyone who will read them. Writing is in your mind, heart, and soul. Since you can't avoid it, you might as well do it to the best of your ability and make a career out of it.

Which is probably why you chose to read this book. Likely you are contemplating becoming a freelance writer. Before reading this book, you wanted to know what to expect in the beginning. You wanted to know what it's like to be a freelance writer. Maybe you had a lot of questions about the specific career and what it entails.

Most of you are probably curious about the money you can make as a freelance writer. I don't blame you. In fact, I wondered about all of these things myself when I first started, and I wished there was a book like this one to turn to. It's comforting to know where you're going before you try something new. That is why I wrote this book. I wrote it for all the talented writers out there who are about to begin their journey as a freelance writer.

One suggestion I have for you is to reach out to other writers. Don't spend all your time trying to make an extra buck. Spend some of your time networking and connecting with other writers and others in the publishing industry who have gone before you and have advice to share with you. Listen to all the advice you can get, and do your research by reading lots of publications on writing. Then make sense of the advice, considering both what the majority says and what your heart says.

A second suggestion is to follow your writer's heart. If something doesn't make sense, don't be afraid to ask questions. You will learn a lot by reading and asking questions. Also, no matter how new to freelance writing you are, share what you've learned. The writing community is huge because of all the knowledge writers have shared with each other. Take a seat amongst it all. Claim your seat in the writing community.

Writers all have one thing in common: they love to write! It is very hard not to do something that you truly want to do. Which is why, if writing is your passion, it is likely your life purpose. Don't deprive yourself of your passion. Don't go against the grain of life by doing something else. Do what is natural for you. Write.

When you are fulfilling your life purpose, you will feel tremendous peace and happiness. You will feel that it is meant to be. You have arrived at what you were meant to do.

So what are you waiting for? Take the next step to become a freelance writer. Then work hard at your craft. The harder you work, the more satisfaction you will feel from your career.

At this point I can't tell you much about what to expect in the future, because I've only been a freelance writer for sixteen months. But I can say that in the last four months doors have opened up for me. I joined a book club and they want to feature all four of my published books. I completed a nonfiction book (this one). I've learned how to organize a blog tour. I've learned how to make book covers. I feel more ingrained in the writing community and more confident about my skills. I have taken up editing other people's writing. I have lots of writer friends throughout the Web—some of whom have taken me under their wing with certain things and some I've flown alongside with. I've also helped new writers by sharing my knowledge and experience gained over my first year of freelance writing.

Where do you want to be in a year? Stuck at the same old boring or stressful job? Or happy and free doing what you love? Because that truly is the difference, and the second one is how I feel now. You *can* make it happen. Do what you have to do. If you need to put money aside from your current job to supplement your income during your first year of freelance writing, do it. Figure out how much you will need and decide on how much you are going to save each month, and stick to the plan. Do you need to talk to your family about your wishes so that some financial adjustments can be made? Then do it. Don't be afraid, and don't put off your dreams any longer. The time to do it is now.

Good luck to you. I hope this guide has reassured you and answered most of your questions. If you have any questions that you would like to ask me, you can reach me by my email address:

christine@christinerice-author.com

Happy writing!

About the Author

Christine Rice has been a freelance writer since 2011, where she has worked for Helium, Yahoo, Suite101, and Textbroker. She writes book reviews for publishers and authors, provides editing services, and manages two blogs. She is the author of three other books: *Poetry for the Heart*, *Essays for the Soul*, and *My Not-So-Ordinary Life*. She is working on her fifth, sixth, and seventh books. She has been writing her whole life and participating in creative writing since the age of ten. Besides writing and editing, she enjoys reading, autumn, dining out, shopping, water, and exercising.

You can find Christine at these places on the Web:

Website:

www.christinerice-author.com

Blog:

www.christinerice-author.com/blog

Facebook:

www.facebook.com/christinerice.professionalwriter

Goodreads:

www.goodreads.com/christine_rice

Twitter:

www.twitter.com/criceauthor

www.ingramcontent.com/pod-product-compliance
Lightning Source LLC
Chambersburg PA
CBHW051457170526
45166CB00001B/282

* 9 7 8 1 4 9 2 2 0 2 0 5 9 *